D0250479

DEFEATING DARK ANGELS

Defeating Dark Angels

*Breaking Demonic Oppression
in the Believer's Life*

Charles H. Kraft

Servant Publications
Ann Arbor, Michigan

Vine Books is an imprint of Servant Publications especially
designed to serve evangelical Christians.

The names and characterizations in this book drawn from the author's
personal experience are rendered pseudonymously and as fictional
composites. Any similarity between the names and characterizations of
these individuals and real people is unintended and purely
coincidental.

Scripture texts used in this work, unless otherwise indicated, are taken
from *Good News Bible: The Bible in Today's English Version*; copyright ©
1976 for Old Testament, American Bible Society, New York; copyright ©
1966, 1971, and 1976 for New Testament, American Bible Society, New
York. The Scripture tests are cited by permission of the copyright owner.

Published by Servant Publications
P.O. Box 8617
Ann Arbor, Michigan 48107

Cover design by Michael Andaloro
Cover Illustration by Martin Soo Hoo

01 02 03 15 14

Printed in the United States of America
ISBN 0-89283-773-X

Library of Congress Cataloging-in-Publication Data
Kraft, Charles H.
  Defeating dark angels : breaking demonic oppression in the
believer's life / Charles H. Kraft with Christy Varney and Ellen
Kearney.
      p. cm.
Includes bibliographical references and index.
ISBN 0-89283-773-X
1. Demonology. 2. Exorcism. I. Varney, Christy. II. Kearney,
Ellen. III. Title.
BF1531.K73 1992
235'.45—dc20   92-15166

Contents

Introduction

WHY FIGHT DARK ANGELS? Because when we do, we receive letters like the following from a young woman I'll call Karen:

I am writing you because I promised to tell you what has occurred in my life. I do not understand all that happened in the time I was ministered to, but after three months there is definite change in my behavior and my attitude and my state of mind, even after trials have come. I give God much thanks and glory because there would be no way that this would be so unless he had done the work!

Since I came back [home]... many, many people have commented on the change in my life, change in my appearance and my countenance.... I had prayed for many years for the work to be done that has been done.

How am I different? Well, first of all, my whole view of God is different. I am no longer afraid of him and can truly say I love him, even though my love for him is imperfect. My view of myself has changed. I truly see myself as having worth in him. I am indeed a princess! I am learning to act as a person of worth. I do not have to fight to be recognized, which I have done all my life. The ugly wound that has plagued my life is healed and I am learning to be a servant. There is peace in my heart.

I've received many letters and verbal statements like this one. And most of them are from people like Karen who faithfully attended a church where it was sincerely believed that Christians could not be demonized. How, then, did they explain her difficulties? They blamed Karen for not working harder at being spiritual. This, of course, made the problems worse and made Karen angry both at herself and at God.

But Jesus wanted Karen free. So he led her to visit a friend who brought her to me. We spent a few hours together—Karen, her friend, Jesus, and I. Most of the time was given to dealing with emotional wounds. But some of those wounds had demons attached to them. And as the Holy Spirit brought healing to the wounds, he also got rid of the demons. There was no spectacle, no violence. Not even any noise. The demons were well entrenched, but the power differential between them and God left them no hope of staying once they were discovered. As with nearly every person I work with, the demons were a minor problem. The major problems were emotional.

But God heals emotional problems. And he banishes any demons that may be feeding on them. The result was that another young woman went free, a young woman who for years had been in captivity to the enemy of our souls. She went free because God can free such people, and because he has taught some of us what to do to help him bring such freedom.

A DIFFERENT PERSPECTIVE ON DEFEATING DARK ANGELS

This book is about defeating dark angels that torment Christians like Karen. It is also about how to work in the power of God to bring freedom with a maximum of love for the afflicted person and a minimum of craziness.

A lot of books are available on dealing with demons and how to get rid of them. And a lot of practitioners on TV join with those books to give the impression that casting out demons is something mystical, only to be attempted by superspiritual, super-anointed specialists with a surplus of emotion and showmanship.

This book is of another sort. Satan and his dark angels are not impressed with showmanship or mystical language and behavior. Indeed, high emotion helps their cause more than God's. For according to Jesus, the task of driving out demons is not simply for specialists. Jesus gave to his disciples, and through them to all of us, "power and authority to drive out all demons and to cure diseases" (Lk 9:1).

I, and the others who have shared my experiences, have been learning some interesting things about how to carry on Jesus' ministry to the demonized. We have learned that today, just as in Jesus' day, getting rid of demons is a normal part of the Christian life for those who would be his disciples. We have also learned that demonization is very common and that deliverance can be done in a loving, often even unobtrusive, way.

This book has been written to share these and other learnings. It doesn't provide all the answers. It may not even ask all the questions. Indeed, I learn so much new each week, it's a shame I can't update the book as I go. I am convinced, however, that general principles exist that someday may add up to a science of dealing with dark angels. And the way to gain understanding ourselves and to help others gain understanding of those principles is by sharing what we have been learning.

I ask, therefore, for the patience of those who know things we don't know. And, that those behind us in learning, plus those using other methods, experiment with the approaches we have found effective. And may God grant you the privilege he has granted us of regularly being involved in freeing people from the Enemy.

WITH THANKS TO THOSE WHO HELPED

I have had much help in developing this book. Among the associates who have taught me are Fred and Susie Heminger;

Molly Sutherland-Dodd; Gary Hixson; Al Reitz; Christy Varney; Ellen Kearney; Bill Stafford; Alex Haarbrink; Marguerite, my wife; and a host of those to whom God has brought freedom through me. I am also grateful to my Fuller faculty colleague, C. Peter Wagner, and his wife Doris, for their encouragement and frequent input as we travel similar paths in power ministry.

For assistance in the actual writing of the book, I would like to express my gratitude to Christy Varney for helping flesh out my original outline. The fact that I could work from her prose rather than simply an outline, speeded this endeavor considerably.

I am grateful also to Ellen Kearney who did most of the collecting and original processing of the twists and turns and the questions in chapters ten and eleven. She also read most of the chapter drafts and made many valuable comments. Her help was especially appreciated, since it came in the final stages of the manuscript as I was trying to meet the deadline.

Thanks are also due my wife, Marguerite, for her patience as I minister to people and sacrifice time with her to write. It is not always easy for her.

Finally, I am deeply grateful to Dave Came, managing editor of Servant Publications, for technical assistance and personal attention to the book. I also thank Oakley Winter who, under Dave's supervision, copy edited the text and Martha Darling who compiled the index.

Biblical quotations are from the Good News translation, unless otherwise indicated. Standard abbreviations are used for the others: New International Version (NIV), Living Bible (LB), Phillips (Phillips).

South Pasadena, CA
January 1992

ONE

Are Satan and Dark Angels for Real?

I N WRITING TO THE EPHESIANS, the Apostle Paul articulated a view of reality that seems strange to even the most sincere of American Christians. He says, "We are not fighting against human beings but against the wicked spiritual forces in the heavenly world, the rulers, authorities, and cosmic powers of this dark age. So put on God's armor now! Then when the evil day comes, you will be able to resist the enemy's attacks; and after fighting to the end, you will still hold your ground" (Eph 6:12-13).

Most Americans who discover the reality of what Paul was talking about, learn it the hard way—by experience. For example, my friend, Ed Murphy, was suddenly "blindsided" by an incident in his family that he could not explain.

DR: ED MURPHY'S CHANGE OF MIND

"Dad, I don't know what's the matter with me. There seems to be something inside of me that takes over at times and makes me do weird things. Dad, help me! I'm scared. I love Jesus and I want to do what is right. What's wrong with me?"

The words were those of Carolyn Murphy, the daughter of Ed Murphy, a respected Christian leader, a vice president of OC Ministries, and former professor at Biola University. Ed has had a worldwide deliverance ministry for some time. When this event happened during the 1960s, however, Ed had only an intellectual belief in demons, though he had been a missionary in Latin America. And he certainly didn't believe that a Christian with as vibrant a faith as that of his fourteen-year-old daughter, could be demonized. Murphy has written an account of his experience with his demonized daughter in the Vineyard Ministries magazine.[1]

Ed had returned home from a trip at the frantic urging of his wife and started talking to Carolyn. "Within moments," Ed recalls,

> her usually sweet personality changed. With a strange glare in her eyes she screamed at me, telling me to leave her alone. There was an undeniably evil presence in her eyes. Carolyn and I went to our knees in prayer, crying to the Lord to break the evil oppressing her life.
>
> I had noticed several weeks before that she had a small round object hanging on a chain around her neck, but didn't think anything of it. As we prayed, my attention was drawn to this object. [She had been given it by a friend who professed Christianity but did not live like a committed believer.]...
>
> After a little investigating, I discovered the "star" to be a pentagram, a symbol of the occult world. "You will not find full freedom from evil spirits until you remove it and renounce the spirit forces associated with it," I told her.
>
> She responded quickly, tearing it off her neck and throwing it on the floor. She confessed and renounced her "innocent" occult involvement and her interest in certain evil rock music. She even confessed to having a selfish and rebellious attitude.
>
> In no time at all, we were in a face-to-face confrontation with evil spirits.

"Dad, they are after me. I'm afraid."

"Get out of my daughter's life," I commanded. "She has broken all allegiance with you. Get out! Leave her alone! In the name and authority of my Master, the Lord, Jesus Christ, who defeated your master on the cross, I command you to go away from Carolyn and don't return. Get out of her life!"

Immediately the struggle ceased. Carolyn became calm, joyfully praising the Lord for setting her free. The evil spirits had left. We both cried and rejoiced before the Lord for his grace.

There was a bit more work to do after this incident, for Carolyn's involvement at the fringes of the hippie-occult subculture turned out to be more than she had at first indicated. However, as she renounced her involvement, confessed her sins, and destroyed the symbols of that way of life (including other "charms" and certain heavy rock music albums), she gained the freedom in Christ she had lost by allowing the Enemy to seduce her.

A RADICAL SHIFT IN UNDERSTANDING

Ed calls it "the most significant worldview shift in my Christian life." Not only did he come to believe in the reality of the dark angels spoken of in Ephesians, he came to realize that even Christians aren't immune to their intrusion. In spite of the warnings in Ephesians and other portions of Scripture (1 Pt 5:8-9; Jas 4:7; 1 Jn 5:19), the position taken by Ed and most evangelicals is that Satan is so defeated (Col 2:15) that his activities can't affect them. They, therefore, believe they don't need to pay much attention to him.

Experiences like Ed's have, however, taught many evangelicals that they were wrong about the Enemy and his dark angels. Though they wish it weren't true, they find that Satan is alive and active, even among those very close to them.

A DELIVERANCE MINISTRY WASN'T PART OF MY LIFE PLAN!

Neither Murphy nor I ever planned to be involved in actually challenging and casting out demons as Jesus did. I suppose nobody plans a life with that expectation. Few things could have been further from my mind, since I wasn't even sure I believed in demons!

Early in my service as a missionary, I was confronted by a Nigerian church leader with the question, "Do you believe in evil spirits?" Though I hedged by answering in the affirmative, I didn't know whether I really believed in them or not. Somehow, though, he and others I worked with perceived I was uncomfortable with the subject, so they didn't raise it often. And during my first five years in Nigeria, I never had to deal with a demon.

But pondering his question, I recalled seeing a section in my seminary theology book on Satan and demons. I think, however, we skipped it! Pressed for time, the professor gave us seminarians the impression that the subject was mainly of historical interest, since Jesus has defeated and humiliated Satan (Col 2:15). So, while we were to accept as fact the existence of Satan and demons, we didn't need to be very concerned with their activities.

In 1982, however, the Lord started showing me otherwise (see Kraft, *Christianity with Power*). To prepare myself for the inevitable, I began reading and quizzing anyone who had experience in deliverance. I read Hammond and Hammond, *Pigs in the Parlor;* Bubeck, *The Adversary* and *Overcoming the Adversary;* Harper, *Spiritual Warfare;* Penn-Lewis, *War on the Saints;* and McAll, *Healing the Family Tree.* I was becoming well-read on the subject, but there's nothing like experience to cement the theory.

The first opportunity to experience a genuine confrontation with demons came early in 1986, after a session of our Signs and Wonders course at Fuller Seminary. A student asked my assistance in praying for an older woman we'll call Claire. She had become stiff and seemingly unconscious while being prayed over. Arriving at the part of the room where their ministry was taking place, I found Claire indeed to be "out of it."

Laying my hand on her shoulder, I spoke "peace" to her. This brought her back to consciousness. But soon she started shaking violently and I found myself challenging a demon in the name of Jesus Christ—just as I had learned from the books. We were able to free her from nineteen demons that evening and one more two days later in my office. And Claire, though already a committed, Spirit-filled and actively ministering Christian, moved into a freedom she had never known.

This was the beginning of a ministry that includes several deliverances in an average week, plus a number of seminars each year, in addition to my regular duties as a professor in the School of World Mission, Fuller Seminary. I didn't plan it that way, but it seems to be what the Lord wants me to do now. Having worked with the Holy Spirit to bring deliverance to more than two hundred Christians—dealing with thousands of demons in the process—I also believe it's time to share with others what God has been teaching me. For he wants many who read this to get involved in just such a ministry.

Deliverance is not among the Bible's list of gifts for believers. Rather, we are *all* to do it (Lk 9:1). But most of us don't know that bringing deliverance is the privilege and responsibility of every Christian. Few experience the joy of seeing people freed from the grip of demons. I pray that this book will supply enough information to allay your fear of challenging the Enemy, increase your confidence in the awesome power of God, develop your boldness to launch out with God in freeing people from demons, motivate you to do the works Jesus promised we would do (Jn 14:12), in the authority and power he has given us (Lk 9:1), and in the process, draw you into a deeper, more intimate relationship with him. *You can be used to bring freedom to demonized people—Jesus said you could.*

People frequently ask me whether I enjoy this kind of ministry. They seem to have the idea that every deliverance is a "knock down, drag out" affair in which all the participants end up beaten and battered. To enjoy something like that strikes them as rather masochistic! So they wonder about me.

Do I enjoy it? Well, I think I really do. But not so much for the process as for the results. Yet the process of openly defeating the Enemy can be a lot of fun too. The crux of the matter is that God really loves people. He loves people so much that he is not satisfied until every bit of the rest Jesus promised in Matthew 11:28, the freedom Paul speaks about in Galatians 5:1, the new creation Paul points to in 2 Corinthians 5:17, is being experienced by his people. And that's what deliverance is all about—bringing people into all of the freedom Jesus desires for his chosen ones.

THE BIBLE TAKES SATAN AND DEMONS SERIOUSLY

The personal experiences of Murphy, myself, and many others serve to authenticate our guidebook, the Bible.

When Jesus started his public ministry, he affirmed the existence of Satan's dark angels by announcing his purpose in the words of Isaiah 61:1-2: "The Spirit of the Lord is upon me, because he has chosen me to bring good news to the poor. He has sent me to proclaim liberty to the captives and recovery of sight to the blind; to set free the oppressed and announce that the time has come when the Lord will save his people" (Lk 4:18-19).

Jesus came to set captives free from the bondage imposed on them by the Enemy, the "ruler of this world" (Jn 14:30), whose aim is to keep people from experiencing the freedom God grants to those who get into a personal relationship with him. Why God allows Satan to continue to torment believers even after their Savior has defeated him at the cross and tomb is a complete mystery to me.

Jesus was affirming a view we see throughout the Old Testament, where we see the evil kingdom constantly lurking in the background and affecting what goes on in the human realm. In the Garden of Eden, the Enemy's activity is obvious. In Job, we see another of Satan's overt challenges to God's authority. In each of Israel's wars, and on each occasion its people follow false gods, both overt and covert interference from the Enemy is apparent.

In the New Testament, we can see Satan behind the plot to kill the baby Jesus (Mt 2:16-18). His activity is overt when he confronts Jesus in the wilderness (Lk 4:1-13) and whenever Jesus cast out demons. He is undoubtedly behind the opposition of the Jewish leaders to Jesus, plus his trial and crucifixion. We see Satan behind many of the events recorded in the book of Acts, for example, Ananias and Sapphira (Acts 5:1-11), and the demonized slave-girl, (Acts 16:16-18). Also, throughout the Epistles, for example, the table of demons (1 Cor 10:21), blinding those who don't believe (2 Cor 4:4), and teachings of demons (1 Tm 4:1). And Satanic activity runs throughout the Book of Revelation.

Satan asserts his authority over the earth when he says to Jesus, "I will give you all this power and all this wealth... It has all been handed over to me, and I can give it to anyone I choose" (Lk 4:6). He is referred to by Jesus as "the ruler of this world" (Jn 14:30), by Paul as "the ruler of the spiritual powers in space" (Eph 2:2), by Peter as one who "roams around like a roaring lion, looking for someone to devour" (1 Pt 5:8) and by John as the one that rules the whole world (1 Jn 5:19).

Despite such statements concerning the impressive position of our Enemy, neither Jesus nor other New Testament characters seemed alarmed by Satan's activities. They dealt with them matter of factly, knowing that God's power is infinitely greater than that of the Enemy.

Scripture makes it clear, however, that Jesus and his followers took demons seriously. While they were not afraid of them, they acknowledged their existence and used the power of the Holy Spirit to fight them. Over and over again, references to demons and Satan's kingdom appear in the Gospels. In the Gospel of Mark, for example, over half of Jesus' ministry is devoted to delivering the demonized.

No one seemed to doubt the existence of demons or the supernatural realm in these biblical accounts. Jesus' critics questioned the source of his power (Lk 11:14-22), but, unlike those influenced by contemporary Western worldviews (see Kraft, *Christianity with Power*), they never questioned the existence of demons who indwelt and harmed people. My own growing experience convinces me they were right and that Paul spoke insightfully when he warned that our real battle is "not against human beings but against the wicked spiritual forces in the heavenly world" (Eph 6:12).

The Bible is clear that Satan has a powerful kingdom that Christians must reckon with at every turn. And we are living in the midst of it—in Enemy territory. To understand demonization, it is critical that we understand Satan's kingdom and how it operates. In Paul's day, he could state, "we know what [Satan's] plans are" (2 Cor 2:11). In our day, we need to be taught the Enemy's strategy if we are to be prepared for battle.

THE SATANIC KINGDOM

Of what does the satanic kingdom consist? At the top is Satan himself. He appears to be a high-ranking angel (perhaps at or near the level of the archangels Michael and Gabriel). He apparently asserted himself in opposition to God, becoming the adversary of all that is good, right, and godly. Though the passages in Isaiah 14:12-15 and Ezekiel 28:11-19 are directed to the kings of Babylon and Tyre, they also appear to describe what happened in the heavenlies when Satan lost his position with God.

In Ezekiel it is said, presumably of Satan, "You were once

an example of perfection.... Your conduct was perfect from the day you were created until you began to do evil" (28:12, 15). In the Isaiah passage, Lucifer (Satan) is described as "determined to climb up to heaven and to place your throne above the highest stars... and be like the Almighty" (14:13-14). Both passages speak of Satan being cast down and humiliated because of his rebellion.

The widely-held belief is that when Satan fell, he took a large number of angels with him. Some interpret Revelation 12:4 as indicating that one-third of the angels in heaven sided with Satan. Though I seriously doubt the validity of that interpretation, there seem to be a *very* large number of satanic beings in the world. And all of them are to be thrown out of heaven with Satan at the end (Rv 12:7-9).

Until God terminates things, however, Satan and his dark angels (demons or evil spirits) will be active on earth. We see from many biblical passages that demons can inhabit people (Mk 1:21; 5:1-20; 7:24; Acts 16:16). Above them there seems to be a hierarchy of principalities and powers (Eph 6:12) working under Satan's authority. Within the hierarchy, these evil beings take orders from those with greater power who rank above them. Release from their assignments, therefore, can only be granted by higher level spirits or by the power of God.

Satanic beings are involved in every kind of disruptive human activity. They can hinder earthly endeavors and even delay answers to prayer (Dn 10:13). They seem to have authority over places and territories, such as buildings, cities, and temples. Additionally, they appear to have authority over social organizations and groups, and influence sinful behavior such as homosexuality, drug addiction, lust, incest, rape, and murder.

The fallen angels we call demons or evil spirits (I make no distinction between those terms) seem to be the "ground level" troops, as opposed to the "cosmic level" principalities, powers, and rulers of Ephesians 6:12. These are the ones we encounter most often during spiritual warfare. Scripture tells us that demons seek people to live in (Mt 12:43-45). They apparently envy us our bodies. They have different personalities, are destructive (Mk 9:17-29), and differ in power and wickedness (Mk 5:4; Mt 12:45).

Satan, unlike God, is not omnipresent. He can only be in one place at a time, though he apparently can get from place to place very quickly. The other members of the hierarchy, including demons, therefore, carry out his schemes throughout the universe. In addition to their broader assignments, it is apparently the task of evil spirits to bother humans, especially Christians. Satan does not like anything that God likes. He, therefore, picks on God's favorite creatures and assigns his underlings to harass us.

We can assume demons' primary concern is to disrupt and, if possible, cripple anything or anyone that might be a threat to Satan's domination over the world. Their guns are aimed at individuals, groups, and organizations that seek to advance God's purposes. They produce "strongholds" in people's minds (2 Cor 10:4) and probably in other places as well. They attack Christian ministries and are agents of doctrinal aberrations (1 Tm 4:1). They affect health (Lk 13:11), perhaps affect weather (Lk 8:22-25), and even have "the power over death" (Heb 2:14), *though they have no power except that allowed them by God.*

THE REALITY OF THE BATTLE

We are at war! Just about every page of the New Testament indicates this fact. As Christians, like it or not, we are participants in the war between the kingdom of God and the kingdom of Satan. Furthermore, we are living in Enemy territory. Fortunately, we are on the winning side! There is absolutely no doubt about the outcome. Not only have the Enemy and his dark angels been defeated, they have been humiliated. For Jesus at his resurrection "made a public spectacle of them by leading them as captives in his victory procession" (Col 2:15). My friend Ken Blue writes, "The fight is real. The victory of Christ through his cross and resurrection is final, but not yet fully realized. Evil continues to exercise its bounded, though significant, power until Christ returns in his glory."[2]

Why we are still at war, I cannot explain. But lags like this between certain victory and the final mop-up are not unknown in history. For example, though about four million slaves were legally freed by the Emancipation Proclamation in 1863, two bloody years of fighting followed before they could claim their freedom in 1865.

A similar kind of delay occurred during World War II. In June of 1944, Allied troops landed successfully on the European mainland, sealing the doom of Hitler and his troops. Though D-day assured the defeat of the Nazis, the war did not end until eleven months later when the Axis signed the unconditional surrender in May 1945. Though victory was assured, more Allied soldiers were killed in Europe during those eleven months than in all the preceding years of World War II.

A third, and in some ways better illustration, comes from the history of Israel. Even before Israel entered the promised land, God had given it to them. It was *their* land. God had given it to Abraham. His promise had been reconfirmed over and over again, and God selected Moses and Joshua to bring the Israelites into the land. But enemies occupied it—formidable enemies who had lived there a long time and would not leave until they were forced out. Though the land belonged to the Israelites, warfare was ahead for them as they crossed the Jordan to take possession of it. They owned the land as soon as God gave it to them but did not possess what was theirs for some time and only then after much struggle.

Just as with the Emancipation Proclamation, D-Day, and God's giving of the land, so with the death and resurrection of Jesus—victory was assured but the Enemy remains at large.

The wrap-up, the final capitulation of the Enemy, the freeing of the remaining prisoners of war, and the banishing and locking up of the Enemy is yet to come. We live in the time between Jesus' Emancipation Proclamation and the freeing of the remaining captives.

The interim period in all these cases was to be used for the ongoing advance into enemy territory. Title to the land is not the same as occupation of it. During the interim time, one group held title, another occupied. The challenge for the group with the title is to take possession of what is legally theirs. But this means the war continues. Battles remain to be fought, territory to be occupied, prisoners to be released.

We Christians live, therefore, in a period of spiritual warfare. We need to be aware of this and to equip ourselves to fight. We dare not assume, as some do, that the territory has been occupied and the power of the Enemy broken.

Jesus said, "As the Father sent me, so I send you" (Jn 20:21). He thus enlisted his followers to join in his commitment to "proclaim liberty to the captives and recovery of sight to the blind; to set free the oppressed" (Lk 4:18). The time had come, he said, to enter the Enemy's territory and to announce that God wants to rescue the people he passionately loves (Lk 4:19). Like Jesus, we need to fight against Satan's kingdom in the power of the Holy Spirit. Most importantly, we need to fight for the same reason that Jesus did—obedience to our Father.

The Bible presents us with the paradox of being on the winning side even as we live in a world where "the loser," Satan, has power. Demons are free to harass and trouble people. Evil continues to abound. I'm often asked, "Why does the Enemy still have so much power over people—even Christians? It doesn't seem fair!" Day after day, people come to me who are wounded by the Enemy. Regularly, I minister to those who have been emotionally, physically, and sexually abused, children who have been demonized—people who have been "beaten up" by the Enemy. It makes me sad and angry to see God's people so deeply hurting and wounded. I don't know why God has given Satan such a long tether (and I often feel angry that I can't explain it). But I do know the battle is real, and I intend to fight, in the power of Jesus, to free people from the Enemy. As Christians, we've been chosen and blessed to be on the winning side! The victory is sure but we are a part of a continuing war.

WHY SHOULD WE SEEK TO UNDERSTAND DEMONIZATION?

"The kind of fasting I want is this: Remove the chains of oppression and the yoke of injustice, and let the oppressed go free.... If you put an end to oppression, to every gesture of contempt, and to every evil word; if you give food to the hungry and satisfy those who are in need, then the darkness around you will turn to the brightness of noon.... You will be known as the people who rebuilt the walls, who restored the ruined houses" (Is 58:6, 9b, 10, 12b).

God desires that Christians work with him to minister to the captives and wounded. When the oppressed are freed, "territory" is taken from Satan, and both God and we who participate in the release share the joy of the freed. As promised in the text quoted above, the darkness around us turns to brightness and we become known as "people who rebuilt the walls, who restored the ruined houses." The call to minister in power—freeing the demonized and healing the wounded—is part of our inheritance as children of God. Not only are healing and joy brought to the ones suffering from attack, but also to those who minister with Jesus.

With a sense of excitement I invite you to join those who have learned to free people from demons in Jesus' name. Let me share with you, quoting from Ken Blue, three reasons we should minister to the demonized:

Initially, I wanted to learn about healing and deliverance to authenticate the gospel in evangelism and carry on effective pastoral care. These original motives were soon joined by others. I found that common human compassion became a compelling reason to pray for the sick. It was also exhilarating to be God's agent in relieving illness and pain. Praying for the sick and seeing them helped was and is intensely gratifying.

Gradually, however, I came to what for me is the essential motive to pray for the sick. I had read the Bible for fifteen years but had never noticed that *when Jesus told his followers to preach the kingdom of God, he also commanded them to heal the sick and cast out demons* (Lk 9:1-2; 10:8-9; Mt 10:7-8; Mk 6:12-13). I preached the gospel because I saw that the Lord commanded this. Now I realized that in the same breath, he also commanded me to heal the sick and cast out demons. Whether or not healing aids in evangelism, or whether or not this ministry is enjoyable or even works, I do not intend ever to stop. *I understand now that the command to pray for the sick is one which I cannot explain away or ignore.*[3] (emphasis mine)

Blue's three reasons are compassion, personal gratification and obedience. We will start with obedience.

1. God expects us to free people. We've seen that the battle is real. We understand that as Christians we are on the winning side. But are we *all* called to minister to the demonized? Are we all called to bring healing to the wounded and to set captives free? Yes, if we seek to be what God wants us to be and to do what he wants us to do.

"If you love me, you will obey my commandments," Jesus said (Jn 14:15), and "If you obey my commands, you will remain in my love, just as I have obeyed my Father's commands and remain in his love" (Jn 15:10). Jesus' ministry was one of obedience to the Father. He provided his disciples with a three-year course of instruction by deed and word concerning how to follow God obediently as he followed him. Declaring, "As the Father sent me, so I send you" (Jn 20:21), he launched the disciples into the world in the power of the Holy Spirit (Acts 1:8), to do and say what he himself modeled.

His teaching of the disciples stressed power ministry, giving them "power and authority to drive out all demons and to cure diseases" and "sending them out to preach the kingdom of God and to heal the sick" (Lk 9:1-2). He later instructed them to teach their own disciples "to obey everything I have commanded you" (Mt 28:20), including the ministry of freeing people from the Enemy.

But, you may be asking, what about gifting? First of all, there is no gift of delivering people from demons. Apparently every believer is empowered to do that without special gifting. Secondly, the list of gifts in 1 Corinthians 12 speaks of "gifts of healings" (v. 9). Evidently, as we obey Jesus' command, we will discover that each of us is gifted in different ways to bring healing to those to whom he has led us. This has certainly been my observation of the people I have seen move in obedience. Those who pray for healing find that God backs them up. But they also vary in effectiveness, with some having greater success with certain ailments than with others.

On the basis of Scripture, experience, and observation, I conclude that *obedience is to precede gifting*. We, like Jesus and his disciples, are to obey God by freeing people from the Enemy. We will discover in that obedience, then, what our special gifting may be. As we obey, God provides my colleagues and myself with the authority, power, and gifting necessary to release people from demons. Those who simply observe, without launching out in obedience, never discover the authority, power, and gifting God gives. These come only as a person moves out with God.

2. A second motivation in deliverance ministry is compassion. Demonization is very common in our world today, whether overseas or in our own country. The Enemy and his emissaries are active and successful in getting into people. A steady stream come to me and my colleagues, far more than we can handle. Sadly, many have found no help either in their churches or from psychologists and counsellors. This isn't because their churches and counsellors don't want to help. They just don't know how. Or are afraid.

Unfortunately, most churches and counsellors lead people to believe that demons don't exist today. They allow those tormented by these evil spirits to believe they are crazy or very sinful, adding further to their pain and guilt. Often demonized persons ask me, "Do you think I'm crazy?" Not infrequently, their pastor or counsellor has given up on them or simply let them keep coming even though nothing has helped. Often, they have lost hope that Jesus can bring healing and freedom.

The statistics are sobering, especially since nearly the same percentages apply to Christians as non-Christians. I have heard it estimated that over 50 percent of Americans under thirty have been physically abused during childhood and over 40 percent of women under thirty have been sexually abused. "Dysfunctional" desribes most American families. It is even probable that a majority of missionaries and pastors, especially those who are younger, also come from dysfunctional homes.

Even more startling is the increase of New Age, satanism, and other occult activities in the United States. New Age centers have been established across the country, especially in resort areas such as Santa Fe, New Mexico, the Colorado mountains, Flagstaff, Arizona, and (as you would expect) many places in California. New Age concepts are infiltrating school curricula. In Los Angeles, for example, a recent third grade experimental curriculum taught the children to call for spirit guides to come help them. Fortunately, the system abandoned it, under pressure. Novelist Frank Peretti details in fictional form a similar case and its results (Peretti, *Piercing the Darkness*).

Blood rituals increasingly are coming to the attention of those who deal with crime. Those involved in these rituals, whether criminals or not, usually are severely demonized. Sadly, the police are often more aware and better informed on these matters than pastors and church leaders. Many are convinced that some type of "evil" is behind much of the gang crimes and drug traffic.

A certain number of Christian converts come out of occult backgrounds. Marvelous conversion experiences prompt them to seek church membership. Unfortunately, we have lost the early church tradition of cleansing new converts of demonic infestation before they join, so they usually come into membership carrying some or all of the demons they once served. Though the demons are weakened because they have lost the spiritual center of the person, they hang on in mind, body, emotions, and will (see chapter three). From those positions they can continue to disrupt both the life of the convert and those to whom the convert relates.

Whether as a result of general dysfunction or occult involvement, the Lord's children are bleeding and broken. They've been attacked by the Enemy throughout their painful lives and many still carry demons. As Christians, we cannot turn these people away. We need to be as compassionate as Jesus, working in his love and power to bring healing and deliverance. Today, possibly more than ever before, it's critical that we learn how to bring the light of Jesus to those in pain and need.

3. A deliverance ministry will increase your faith in Jesus. All of us who have moved in this direction have experienced tremendous renewal in our own spiritual lives. *It is an incredible thing to be involved constantly in doing what we know we cannot do.* We cannot cast out demons by ourselves. If the Holy Spirit doesn't "show up" to do the job, we're sunk! So, the very fact that demons are regularly cast out, never to return, constantly humbles, excites, and enriches us. It proves over and over again that God actually is present and doing his work through us.

When the Lord pours out his Holy Spirit on the wounded, he splashes blessings on everyone else too. It's like getting too close to a waterfall! You get sprayed just being there! Through this ministry, my life has been dramatically changed and God has become much bigger! I have felt personally for the first time an answer to Paul's prayer that his readers will experience the "incomparably great power" available to "us who believe" (Eph 1:19, NIV). As I've sought to walk in obedience in this ministry, the Lord has led me deeper and deeper into intimacy with Jesus and excitement over my relationship with him.

Such a fact should come as no surprise. Doesn't God often work in that way? The Lord is not simply concerned with what we are doing for him. As with the apostles, he chose us first to "be with him," and only then to go witness and cast out demons (Mk 3:14-15). His primary concern is for our relationship with him. So step out in obedience to "loose the chains of injustice, and untie the cords of the yoke, to set the oppressed free and break every yoke" (Is 58:6, NIV). As you do you will receive enormous blessing and "Then you will call, and the Lord will answer; you will cry for help, and he will say: Here am I" (Is 58:9, NIV). This ministry benefits not only the demonized, it benefits you too! Jesus desires for you to know the incredible joy of seeing him move in power through you.

HOW TO GET STARTED

A main purpose of this book is to get others started in this important ministry. The number of Christians who need to be freed from demons is alarming. I have no idea how high to estimate the percentages, but I will risk criticism and suggest that in many churches, at least a third of those who attend carry demons.

What if my figure is high? Or low? How many demonized people do you think it would take to cripple a church? Half the membership? I doubt it. One or two in prominent positions? That's probably enough. The pastor? Or the music director? Our experience leads us to believe many in church leadership positions carry demons. Many come to us.

If you were Satan, on whom would you spend your time? What kind of priority would Satan likely give to disrupting the lives and ministries of church people? High priority, I should think. For these are the ones who could hurt the satanic kingdom if they got free.

My point is, there is a lot of work to do with today's equivalent of "the lost sheep of the house of Israel" (Mt 15:24; 10:6). And many of God's people need to learn how to minister freedom to them, if the church is to become what Jesus intended it to be.

To move into this ministry, here are steps I, and those who work with me, have been following:

1. We began by praying, letting God know we were open to whatever he chose to bring our way. We prayed for opportunities to engage in Jesus' freeing ministry, and for the necessary guidance, authority, and power.
2. We read everything we could get our hands on, listened to tapes, attended seminars, and discussed deliverance with anyone with experience. We continue in these activities because there is still much to learn.
3. We sought opportunities to participate with those ministering deliverance, learning by watching and helping. We continue to minister with others, even after we have begun to lead ministry. Working with others as they lead enables us to learn constantly from each other.
4. We then began to offer seminars to a variety of church groups, sharing with them what we have been discovering. I have been the primary teacher to this point, but others are now teaching very effectively. Important to

our instruction is the fact that we demonstrate as well as lecture. Bringing people to freedom in Christ and teaching others how to do likewise requires that we imitate the Master. He not only talked, he did the works as well.

We conduct seminars as a group, with one or more of us speaking and each of us ministering. Those attending watch and, as much as possible, participate. We want them to learn to do what Jesus and we do, not simply to be able to talk about it.

5. We regularly share with each other what we are learning both in seminars and in our individual ministries. Each of us is led by the Spirit to do different things with the result that each of us has a distinctive style. This enables us to provide insight and learning for one another.

WHAT NEXT?

Read on to learn more about what God has helped us discover. Read other books as well (see the bibliography). And listen to teaching tapes—mine and those of others. But remember that deliverance is only a part of the overall aim of getting people well. People need to be completely freed, physically, emotionally, and spiritually. So read, too, on physical healing and in the area usually referred to as "inner healing," or "healing of the memories." One who ministers to a person needs to be equipped to deal with every aspect of that person.

Along with the reading and listening, practice, practice, practice!

TWO

Twelve Myths Concerning Demonization

"The Spirit of the sovereign LORD is on me
because the LORD has anointed me,
to preach good news to the poor.
He has sent me to bind up the brokenhearted,
to proclaim freedom for the captives
And release from darkness for the prisoners."   **Is 61:1-2, NIV**

A DEMONIZED PASTOR

I was discussing demonization with a couple of pastors during a seminar lunch break. The topic was quite unfamiliar to them. One of them I'll call George, began to share with us a lifelong problem he had had with fear. Though George had been in counseling for some time, his fear had not been overcome. Indeed, he said, he was highly anxious at that very moment. After a silent prayer, I looked straight at George saying, "If there's a spirit of fear here, I command you to leave, in the name of Jesus."

Shock was on George's face as I looked directly at him but talked "past him" to the demon inside. For a pastor who wasn't sure he believed in such things, the approach seemed awfully direct, and I seemed overly confident in my diagnosis of what lay behind his problem. Then amazement filled George's face as he said over and over, "The fear is gone! The fear is gone!"

Though psychologists and others may try to explain naturalistically what happened, my interpretation is that something inside George responded to my command to leave. What hadn't happened when psychological principles were applied, happened immediately after a single command. That is, when I treated the problem as if an evil being was behind it, and commanded that being to leave in Jesus' name, the fear vanished. And it has not recurred.

As I mentioned in chapter one, not long ago I would only have been able to offer George my sympathy, and recommend he continue getting psychological help. However, I have since had so many experiences similar to this that I have come to believe that demons do exist, that they live in people, and they frequently are responsible for harassment not unlike what George was experiencing.

My theory is that a fairly weak demon was living within him, whose assignment was to use fear to hamper his effectiveness as a servant of Christ. My analysis is that the demon did not *cause* the fear. Talking with the pastor, I discovered he had experiences in early childhood that predisposed him to fearfulness. This weakness allowed the demon in during his early life, providing the "food" on which the demon fed to keep him off balance. I think the demon had been very greatly weakened as the pastor dealt with the problem through counseling. All that remained, then, was for the demon to be banished once and for all. And that seemed to happen that day at lunch (in a restaurant, by the way).

As a footnote to this story, it is interesting to note the reaction of the other pastor. He first indicated surprise, then what I will call "fearful skepticism." He was not used to being in situations he could not explain. So he attempted to find a naturalistic explanation that would restore his composure and give him a sense of control over what he had just witnessed.

George's description of how he felt inside, however, would not allow the second pastor to explain things away. Once the second pastor accepted the validity of George's experience, though, he became fearful that if his friend was carrying a demon, perhaps demons were all around and in some of the rest of us as well. Perceiving this, I asked him, "If there are demons, would you rather know or not know of their existence and activities?" He replied, "I'd rather not know!"

Why do many of us respond to the thought of demons in this way? These were pastors, well-acquainted with the Scriptures. But they were also Westerners who had imbibed with their "mother's milk" a naturalistic understanding of reality. They found it easy to regard accounts of demonization as biblical events that no longer happen, since Westerners don't believe in invisible spiritual beings. Or, if such beings exist, they occur only overseas, not in "Christian" America. Or, at least, we need not concern ourselves with them, since "He who is in us is greater than he who is in the world" (1 Jn 4:4, Phillips). One way or the other, many Christians remain ignorant of the Enemy, his helpers, and their schemes (2 Cor 2:11).

Or, confronted with the possibility that demons are indeed all around, a typical evangelical response is that of the second pastor—fear, accompanied by a strong desire to engage in "flight rather than fight"! This fear results from becoming aware of the presence of the demonic world, but not knowing what to do about it. Usually mixed in is a heavy dose of misconceptions (encouraged by the Enemy) concerning how to deal with this area of reality. One thing that bothered the second pastor, for example, was the matter-of-fact way I dealt with the problem, even in a restaurant. If it was really a demon wouldn't it have created a scene? he was wondering. And don't you have to go through a lot of religious ritual, such as prayer and fasting, before you challenge them?

Most evangelicals live in profound ignorance as well as fear in this regard. Neither is necessary. We don't know everything, but enough understanding is available for us to make a good start. Let's begin by dispelling myths that surround the subject. Many are among Satan's favorite lies!

MYTH 1: CHRISTIANS CANNOT BE DEMONIZED

This is one of Satan's favorites. If he can get Christians to believe it, his demons can work freely within those Christians and their churches.

Prominent Christian leaders perpetuate this myth. At least one whole denomination holds to this belief (see Reddin, *Power Encounter*). Their doctrine assumes that since the Holy Spirit lives within a Christian, a demon cannot also live there —an assumption that they unconsciously employ when interpreting the Bible and human experience. Though those who believe this myth may claim it is founded on biblical truth, it is in reality, based on an assumption, and they are interpreting the Bible accordingly.

Such an unexamined assumption is very dangerous because it keeps those who believe it from investigating other possibilities. They, therefore, never consider the possiblity of a demon in a Christian, no matter how obvious it may be. Or, should the evidence of a demon become clear even to them, their assumption forces them to deny that the demonized person is a Christian. So the person feels doubly condemned—for having a demon and for not truly having accepted Christ.

I often wish such skeptics could follow me around for a few weeks and listen to the testimonies of the Christians before we get their demons out and listen to them again after they have been delivered. Those who have honestly looked at the evidence have changed their assumption—for example, MerrillUnger, Murphy, and most of the rest of us. In the face of the overwhelming evidence, the burden of proving otherwise rests on the skeptics. They will have to take seriously the evidence in a way not done in supposedly definitive works like Opal Reddin's *Power Encounter*. Once they have taken that evidence seriously, they will have to either agree that Christians can be demonized or develop some pretty sophisticated theory to explain the phenomena of demonization in Christians' lives.

However, those who assume Christians cannot be demonized are partly right. *A demon cannot live in the Christian's spirit—that is, the person's central core, the part that died when Adam sinned,* because Jesus now lives there. Demons can, however, live in other parts, just as sin can. For some, the process of battling the Enemy as they grow in Christ involves battling indwelling demons as well as overcoming sinfulness within. A more detailed refutation of this myth is in the following chapter.

MYTH 2: PEOPLE ARE "POSSESSED" BY DEMONS

The term "demon possessed" is commonly used to describe a person with demons living inside. This comes from the poor rendering in many Bible translations of the Greek word *daimonizomai*. In older translations and even in the NIV, this word is rendered "demon possessed."

Please bear with the technicalities in the following paragraphs. It is important that we not be sloppy in translation when the issue is the amount of credit given to Satan. For what Satan is able to do to people is seriously overestimated by the use of the word "possession."

The word *daimonizomai* occurs seven times in Matthew, four times in Mark, once in Luke, and once in John. A parallel expression, *echein daimonion,* "have a demon," occurs once in Matthew, three times in Luke, and five times in John. Luke uses the latter phrase interchangeably with *daimonizomai*. Though the scriptural authors may have intended that *daimonizomai* indicate a slightly greater degree of demonic control than *echein daimonion,* translators simply are not justified in rendering either term "demon possession." This rendering signifies too much control. Both wordings are better translated "have a demon" (see, for example, Mt 4:24; 8:16, 28, 33; 9:32; 12:22; 15:22 in GNB).

It is critical that the relationship between demons and those in whom they reside be stated accurately. *The word "possessed" greatly overstates the influence wielded by the vast majority of demons.* One might make a case for using that word to describe extreme cases (for example, the Gadarene demoniac of Mt 8:28-34). But it is misleading and harmful to so label the many people battling the lesser influence demons more commonly have. I would estimate at less than 10 percent the number of cases where demons exert control that could be termed possession.

It is far better to use a more neutral term such as "have a demon" or "demonized." Both are more true to the original Greek and also run less risk of frightening people. To quote Unger:

> The term "demon possession" does not appear in the Bible. Apparently it originated with the Jewish historian, Flavius Josephus, in the first century A.D. and then passed into ecclesiastical language. The New Testament, however, frequently mentions demoniacs. They are said to "have a spirit," "a demon," "demons," or "an unclean spirit." Usually such unhappy victims of evil personalities are said to be "demonized" (*daimonizomenoi*), i.e., they are subject to periodic attacks by one or more inhabiting demons, who derange them physically and mentally during the seizure!¹

These more neutral terms do not give more credit to Satan than his due. They also enable us to recognize the differing levels of demonic influence and to indicate demonic strength more accurately. For example, if we say that Pastor George, mentioned earlier, was demonized, but that the strength of his demon was about a "one" on a scale from 1–10, we get a very different picture than if we say he was demon possessed. As a matter of fact, he was far from "possessed" by what was a very weak spirit of fear. He was constantly troubled but not possessed because his demon did not have the strength to take complete control (possession) of him. The demon was indeed at about a level one, on the scale I'll describe in chapter six.

Nearly all contemporary writers on demonization prefer the terms "demonized" and "demonization" in place of "demon possessed" and "demon possession" (see Unger, *Demons in the World Today* and *What Demons Can Do to Saints;* and Dickason—despite the mistitle, *Demon Possession and The Christian;* White, *The Believer's Guide to Spiritual Warfare;* Wagner, *Engaging the Enemy;* and Wimber, *Power Healing*). I also prefer to avoid imprecise terms such as "affliction," "oppression," or "bondage" to describe the condition of persons inhabited by demons, though they may be useful labels for demonic influence operating from outside a person.

Experience leads me to believe that demons cannot totally control a person all the time, though in severe demonization, nearly total control may occur for shorter or longer periods of time. In such cases, however, "severe demonization" is preferable to "demon possessed." As noted earlier, a demon can *never* completely control a Christian, because it cannot live where Jesus is in the person's spirit. This reality will be discussed in more detail in chapter three.

MYTH 3: DELIVERANCE IS A ONE-SHOT DEAL

I'm often asked, "It seems like Jesus commanded demons to leave and they left immediately. Why doesn't this happen when we try to do it?" Many Christians who have attempted to free people from demonization become frustrated because it doesn't seem to be as easy as it was for Jesus.

I wish I had a good answer for them. The truth is, I can only guess. Sometimes (as with Pastor George) I have invoked the power of Jesus and the demon has left immediately. In one case, as soon as I challenged the demon, he said, "Just get me out of here!" I simply commanded him to leave, and he did. In another, after a very short time the demon said, "I don't like this! I'm leaving, and I'm going to take all my friends with me!" So all I had to say was, "Go ahead." And they left. In such cases, however, we need to be sure we follow up with whatever inner healing is necessary to enable the person to prevent the possibility of further demonic invasion.

Usually, however, deliverance takes longer, especially with an approach such as ours, that deals with the emotional and spiritual "garbage." I often wonder if and how Jesus dealt with such garbage. Paul indicates in Ephesians 4:17-5:20 that similar emotional and spiritual problems existed in the first century.

On at least three occasions, Jesus' healings and deliverances appear not to have been immediate. In dealing with the Gadarene demoniac (Mk 5:1-15), verse eight records the fact that Jesus *was commanding* the demons to leave. A process was involved. Likewise, in healing the blind man at Bethsaida (Mk 8:22-26), the Master had to touch his eyes a second time because his sight was only partially restored after the first touching. And then there is the experience of the disciples who could not get a demon out (Mk 9:18) because, as Jesus said, "Only prayer can drive this kind out" (Mk 9:29).

Deliverance is very seldom a one-shot deal, in my experience. I would gladly do things more quickly if I could. But, for reasons I don't fully understand, that's not the way it happens for me. What does happen, though, is that people are marvelously freed from the satanic beings inside them. And that makes it all worth it.

I suspect the difference between my effectiveness and that of Jesus, is that Jesus had perfect intimacy with the Father and did only what he saw the Father doing (Jn 5:19). Because of his complete intimacy with the Father, Jesus always worked at full power, full authority, and with perfect timing. I'm quite sure I don't, and am frequently amazed at God's willingness to use me nonetheless.

Jesus spent hours alone with the Father, receiving authority and instructions for the next steps in his ministry. He then ministered only to those the Father pointed out to him. Jesus must have passed by hundreds of people who were sick, emotionally wounded, or demonized. But he didn't choose to heal everyone—only those the Father chose for him. As was the case with Jesus, then, deeper intimacy with God should be our first priority. Presumably, if we could hear his voice and obey him as completely as Jesus did, we would be able to do Jesus' works in the way he did them.

However, this side of heaven we will not achieve perfect intimacy with the Father and, therefore, will be deficient in power, authority, and timing. For this reason, I have taken the position along with my friend, Ken Blue, that "Whether or not this ministry [of healing and deliverance] is enjoyable or even works, I do not intend to ever stop. I understand now that the command to pray for the sick is one which I cannot explain away or ignore."[2]

Jesus' command is to be obeyed, even if our deliverances take longer than those of Jesus, and even if our intimacy with the Father is not that of Jesus. The freedom that Jesus brings to others and the exciting enrichment he brings into our lives through this ministry make it a thousand times worthwhile. To be allowed to work in the power of God is an incomparable privilege. This is a power far beyond our power, enabling us to do the things Jesus promised we would do (Jn 14:12) even though we know we cannot do them! I never plan to quit. It's too much fun to see freed people smile!

MYTH 4: DEMONIZATION IS SIMPLY PSYCHOLOGICAL ILLNESS

Liberal Christians assume that the biblical accounts of Jesus casting out demons simply record Jesus' way of dealing with psychological illness. "Jesus simply accommodated to the belief of the people of that day that demons caused problems," they say. "He knew then what we know now—that the so-called demonized were really heavy-duty psychological cases."

Unfortunately, variations of this myth are common among evangelicals as well. Our naturalistic Western worldview (see Kraft, *Christianity with Power*) makes it extremely difficult for us to believe supernatural beings such as Satan and demons are real. We are taught as we grow up that "seeing is believing" and "if you can't see it, it doesn't exist." Invisible beings with power are all right in fairy tales, but they have no place in real life.

Furthermore, we are so impressed with Western scientific thought, including psychology, that it seldom occurs to us that our scientists may not always have the correct explanation for such phenomena. Most Westerners cannot handle the possibility that scientists and scholars do not have a better understanding of demonization than the people of the first century. When we come in contact with persons acting like the demonized people of the Gospels, we take them to psychologists, even though recent studies question the ability of psychological counseling to bring healing in extreme cases.

So we question "spiritual" interpretations of the demonization passages, rather than question the correctness of our Western worldview. Those of us who have been "blasted" out of our naturalistic worldview assumptions in this area, however, have no doubt that we cannot reduce demonic phenomena to psychological phenomena. Nor can we regard all psychological phenomena as demonic. They are distinct and to consider them one and the same is a myth.

MYTH 5: ALL EMOTIONAL PROBLEMS ARE CAUSED BY DEMONS

In reaction to myth four, many who discover that demons really exist often go to the opposite extreme. They begin to believe that all emotional problems (and most others as well) are caused by demons. This is the "lunatic fringe" position of many Pentecostals and charismatics. And it turns off large numbers of both Christians and non-Christians to even considering the possibility that demons exist and are active.

Though I contend that demonization is very common, it is clear to me that emotional problems are seldom if ever *caused* by demons. The origin of such difficulties lies elsewhere. When a child is abused, for example, though a demon may be pushing the abuser, *it is the abuse, not the demon, that causes the problem in the child.* The child may or may not become demonized as a result of that abuse. The emotional hurt is one thing, the demonization, if there be any, is another. I have dealt with quite a number of persons severely abused as children who have not contracted demons. I have dealt with many others who have.

As I point out under the next myth, Satan and demons are sterile and, therefore, cannot create anything from nothing. They can only piggyback on what is there already. Whether or not any given problem involves their piggybacking on it must be tested. *We cannot simply assume that every problem has been caused by demons. That is too simplistic.*

I have no idea what percentage of problems involve demons. My impression is that though most are not initiated by demons, demons are involved at least indirectly in the majority. Whether or not that is accurate, I think we can assume that demons affect many things, acting from either inside or outside of persons. As we will see in chapter five, most of their work is from the outside.

Their ability to *cause* is, I believe, limited to whatever influence they can have on persons and events. Demons are, however, very opportunistic. If, for example, abuse occurs even without demonic initiative, they are eager to make it worse. Or, if things are going well for a person, they will do whatever they are permitted to do to push the person to ignore, exaggerate, or divert those good things.

Demons need to be seen, then, not only in terms of their presence but also in terms of their strategies and limitations.

Two major limitations that we will constantly refer to are the power of God and the strength of the human will. Demons cannot stand against the power of God, when activated, or a strong human will. And when a strong human will is empowered by God and directed against them, it is impossible for them to win. When, however, that will, though potentially empowered by God (as in the case of every Christian) is in a person who lacks understanding in this area, demonic enemies can play games with the will that give the person the impression of not being able to handle temptations and attacks.

To ignore the activities of demons is folly. But to give them more credit than they are due is also folly.

MYTH 6: SUCH PROBLEMS ARE EITHER DEMONIC OR EMOTIONAL

Americans have what may be called an "either-or" mentality. We also tend to look for simple answers. This leads many to assume symptoms of the kind we have been discussing, are *either* demonic *or* emotional. Thus, those with a naturalistic mentality attempt to see such problems as emotional, while those who are more aware of the spirit world, want to blame them on demons. Still others who believe problems can be both demonic and emotional, want to divide them into one or the other.

However, to believe such problems can be categorized into one or the other is a myth. They cannot be neatly divided into exclusively emotional or exclusively demonic. Experience teaches us that:

1. People may have emotional problems but not demons, and
2. People may have emotional, physical, or spiritual problems and *also* demons.

Demons cannot create anything from nothing. They, like Satan, are sterile. They can only work on what already is.

Emotional or spiritual problems provide the garbage that attracts the demonic rats. But not all emotional garbage is sufficient to attract them. Thus, many with symptoms of emotional illness are simply emotionally ill. But others with similar symptoms may suffer from both emotional illness and demonization.

Since this is true, it is extremely important that we not simply look for demons or, when demons are discovered, deal with only the demonic problem. The aim is to bring healing at whatever level necessary. If the problems are simply emotional, we treat the person accordingly. If however, they are both emotional and demonic, we deal with both.

Whether or not there are demons, emotional problems are primary. Demonization is always secondary, just as rats are secondary to garbage. If we get rid of the rats and keep the garbage, the person is in great danger still. But if we get rid of the garbage, what we have done automatically affects the rats. *Whether there are demons or not, therefore, we go after the primary problem—the emotional and spiritual garbage.*

Unlike other deliverance ministries, then, I do not divide people into the demonized and the emotionally ill for the purpose of treating one group one way and the other, another. Instead, I assume that emotional problems are to be treated as emotional problems, whether or not there are also demons, and that we should deal with them first. If the person turns out also to have demons, we deal with them after the demons' "food" (the emotional problems) has been greatly reduced. By that time any demons still there will be much weaker than if we had challenged them at the beginning. This approach recognizes that *the real problem facing demonized people is never the demons, but the deep-level emotional problems to which they are attached.*

Because of this approach, we don't consider our ministry simply a "deliverance ministry." Deliverance is never a "simple" process where one goes after demons and that's the end of it. The "important stuff" is the emotional woundedness that has allowed demons to enter a person. These emotional problems must be addressed through inner healing prayer and sound Christian counseling. The combination of inner healing prayer, deliverance, and solid Christian therapy is often the key to wholeness for the demonized. This is especially true for the severely abused—for example, satanic ritual abuse victims.

MYTH 7: DEMONIZATION IS UNCOMMON IN THE UNITED STATES

I am often asked by church leaders why we in the United States need to learn about deliverance. They believe that our country has been so thoroughly influenced by Christianity that the Enemy couldn't be a serious threat here. Unlike many other Americans, these people believe in demons, but are deceived in several ways. First, they assume that the Christian influence in America has been sufficient to thwart demonization. Second, they assume that demonization will be obvious. Third, based on that assumption, they further assume that demonic activity occurs only where it is obvious, such as in other societies. They assume that Satan is intelligent enough not to use demonization here, but it doesn't occur to them that he is clever enough to work evil in a less obvious manner than they have assumed is required.

This common myth is extremely damaging. The Enemy is delighted to see so many Christian leaders, churches, and believers buy into this lie. The truth is, the United States is far from free of demonic influence. For those who are open to seeing them, the Enemy's fingerprints are all around. Let those who have eyes observe the following:

1. Nearly all American cities have a variety of occult establishments. In them satanic power is used and passed on by people called palmists, fortune tellers, psychics, tarot

card readers, and astrologers. Spiritists, scientologists, and psychics advertise openly. In addition, people can pick up demons in older establishments, such as Masonic temples, Christian Science churches, Mormon and Jehovah's Witness meeting places. Buddhist and Islamic temples are springing up. *Karate* and *Tai Chi* instructors regularly commit themselves and their students to evil spirits.

2. The Christian world often seems less knowledgeable about the reality of spiritual evil than the secular. *Time Magazine* has featured articles on evil (June 10, 1991) and on non-orthodox medical practitioners (November 4, 1991). The latter described several occult approaches to healing that would likely result in demonization. Indeed, the influence of the New Age movement, meditation, and other occult practices in the area of healing is very great. So many health food shops are infected that we would be well advised to claim God's protection whenever we enter one. In addition, curricula in some elementary schools teach children to link up with spirit guides, or demons.

3. The print and electronic news media assault viewers with reports of ritual killings and abuse, such as: the satanic symbols and language of serial killer Richard Ramirez ("The Night Stalker"); the satanic cult involvement of mass murderers Richard Berkowitz (Son of Sam) and Henry Lee Lucas; satanists on the *Geraldo* show; alleged sexual abuse in child care centers; and the ritual death of a family along the Texas-Mexico border. These perk our ears up and make us wonder what else is going on that we don't hear about. Startling accounts of the activities of satanists (see Larson, *Satanism*), and devotees of New Age (see Groothuis, *Unmasking the New Age* and *Confronting the New Age;* Chandler, *Understanding the New Age)* should cause us to sit up, take notice, and do some-

thing about the problems. For Americans are choosing to become demonized at what is probably a more rapid rate than ever before.

James Friesen, a Christian psychologist who specializes in dealing with multiple personality disorder, provides some sobering statistics in his recent book, *Uncovering the Mystery of MPD.* He reports that at least a hundred thousand people in the United States have been subjected to satanic ritual abuse as children. Even more disturbing is the finding of the Los Angeles Task Force on Ritual Abuse, that over one hundred California pre-schools have been implicated in ritual abuse. Friesen quotes another source as saying, "From the number of preschool cases alone, it would appear that a massive indoctrination of American children into Satanism is going on."[3] Most such crime, however, goes unpunished (Friesen documents several examples), largely because good people won't believe it is happening and do something about it.

Demonic activities *are* occurring throughout the United States. Furthermore, most people are shocked to learn that those involved in the satanic and occult aren't stereotypical "gang-like" individuals. Most behave quite normally in ordinary life. Many are socially prominent and well-respected, such as doctors, teachers, and lawyers. They sometimes even use church facilities for their rituals.

There are at least three good reasons for reporting this information. First, it is happening on a large scale in our country and we need to adjust our belief system to accept this fact. Second, adults who participate in such rituals, and children who are abused in them, become demonized. Third, the Church of Jesus Christ needs to wake up and put to work its unique power to free victims. Demonization is not simply a problem for missionaries working in other countries. "The whole world is under the rule of the Evil One," including America (1 Jn 5:19). And as Friesen says, "Evil will spread when good people do nothing."[4]

MYTH 8: THOSE WITH DEMONS ARE GUILTY OF SPIRITUAL REBELLION

Much damage is done to a person suffering from demonization when well-meaning Christians suggest it is because they are sinful and rebellious. Jesus never blamed people for having demons. That demonization comes about only through conscious choice is a lie. As we will see, conscious choice is but one way, and comparatively rare among Christians.

As someone has pointed out, we Christians are good at shooting our wounded. Those suffering from demonization are already in deep pain and confusion; implying that their problem is their own fault makes their plight even worse. Many to whom I have ministered have come to me with great shame, fearing that their turmoil indicates a major, perhaps even unforgivable, problem in their relationship with God.

These demonized Christians are, almost without exception, anything but rebellious to Christ or wallowing in sin. Rather, they are courageous believers who deeply love Jesus, but can't explain or free themselves from something that has a hold on their lives. Teri is typical. Whenever she participated in worship an intense battle went on inside her. The compulsion to get up and run was well-nigh overpowering.

It was obvious both from observing Teri's life and hearing her descriptions of her quiet times with the Lord, that she was deeply committed to Jesus. Since I know that demons hate worship, I suspected the interference she was experiencing might be demonic. After dealing with several "garbage" issues in Teri's life, largely related to self-esteem, Jesus used me to evict several fairly weak demons. Teri now worships wholeheartedly without interference.

A pastor I'll call Paul came to me very hesitantly, admitting he had been hearing voices in his head since childhood. Paul's sense of guilt was high, since he believed something was wrong with his spiritual life if the voices in his head came from demons. Indeed, he was convinced that if the voices were those of demons, he would be disqualified from continuing in the ministry. However, we were able to establish that the demons had come to him through inheritance (see chapter three) and that, therefore, he need carry no guilt for their presence. Today, having experienced Jesus' power to deliver him, he is free from both the demons and the guilt.

Rebellious persons seldom come for deliverance. Those who do have been deeply wounded or abused. Their great pain, through little or no fault of their own, has opened the door to a demonic presence in their lives. Usually they have been abused during childhood, often by family members whom they trusted and wanted to please. Sometimes the abuse has had a satanic or ritual dimension. When people become demonized through abuse or inheritance, it is totally unchristian to suggest it was their fault. *They were victims and, in accordance with some law of the universe, they became demonized.*

Even persons who have contracted demons during rebellion do not need guilt added to their already heavy load. That is not Jesus' way. Both Carolyn and Teresa, whose stories are in chapters one and three, invited in demons during times of rebellion—Teresa consciously, Carolyn unconsciously. For each of them, however, the sweetness of their relationship with Jesus was too precious for them to want to remain permanently under the influence of the invited demons, so they sought deliverance. Jesus' way is not to condemn even bad choices. Though their condition was the result of rebellion, they are not to be treated in terms of that rebellion, but according to their desire to be free. And Jesus graciously freed them both, without condemnation.

It is cruel to add to the wounds of demonized people. What they need is Jesus' love and power to bring freedom both from demons and any guilt coming from inside themselves or from the Christian community. Besides deliverance, they need to trust the truth in John 8:32, that they need bear little or no responsibility for their condition, and that whatever responsibility they do bear, can be forgiven. "Therefore, there is now no condemnation" (Rom 8:1, NIV), even for those afflicted with demons.

MYTH 9: ONLY THOSE WITH "SPECIAL GIFTING" CAN CAST OUT DEMONS

Many Christians believe that casting out demons can only be done by those who are very spiritual and have "special deliverance gifts." They believe that only those who have a "gift of deliverance" or a special anointing for deliverance should be allowed to minister to the demonized. Satan loves this myth, because when people believe it, they don't even attempt deliverance.

However, the Scriptures do not speak of a gift of deliverance! In none of the lists of spiritual gifts in the New Testament (1 Cor 12-14; Rom 12:1-8; Eph 4:1-16; 1 Pt 4:7-11) is deliverance included. Some disagree over whether deliverance is implied in the gifts of healing, miracles, or discernment, yet deliverance as such was never singled out. I believe this is because all believers have the authority to cast out demons.

On earth, Jesus worked in the power of the Holy Spirit to free people from demons. He then gave his disciples (first the twelve, then the seventy-two) authority to cast out demons (Lk 9, 10). Later, he gave the disciples the Holy Spirit (Jn 20:22), the same power Jesus worked under to do his mighty works, and commanded the disciples to teach their followers "to obey everything I have commanded you" (Mt 28:20). I take this to mean that all of us who, like the disciples, have both received the Holy Spirit and been taught to obey Jesus' commands, are to cast out demons, whether or not we feel specially gifted for the task.

Since we all have been given the Holy Spirit, we know the power is ours. And since we, like the disciples, have been given authority by Jesus, we know we have the right to cast out demons. All we need do is use what already has been given to each of us. Deliverance is a matter of obedience, not gifting.

While all believers have authority and power, then, it is important to recognize that special gifting can be extremely helpful. That is to say, while a specific deliverance gift isn't required for deliverance ministry, God has given the listed spiritual gifts to enable his church to bring freedom to the oppressed. It is very helpful, for example, to have on a ministry team those with gifts such as: word of wisdom, word of knowledge, discernment, healing, miracles, mercy, and prophecy.

We rejoice in God-given spiritual gifts to his church and affirm that these gifts can and should be used to convey much insight and power in a deliverance ministry. God does indeed give spiritual gifts to help set captives free, but specific gifts are not required to minister to the demonized. The only qualification for a deliverance ministry is a humble, willing group of Christian people who, under the authority of Jesus, desire to bring healing and freedom to the oppressed.

There is, however, the question of how people become proficient in a deliverance ministry, or any other healing ministry. As I have written elsewhere concerning my entrance into a healing ministry, "Perhaps the biggest surprise for me, once I got started, was the need for learning and experimenting. I had always assumed that people received the 'gift' of healing all at once. But what I have experienced is a gradual learning process that comes along with constant practice and a lot of risk-taking."[5]

People who watch me minister to demonized people often make statements like, "It seems so easy when you do it. I'm not sure I can now or will ever be able to do that." My reply is usually something like, "I understand. It was only a few years ago that I was in your place, struggling with discouragement as I watched the experts minister. 'Will I ever be able to work so smoothly and confidently?,' I remember wondering. The answer, after a lot of practice, is 'Yes.'"

By now, I've had the privilege of helping quite a number move from "zero" to impressive competence—some greater than mine. I've seen very few who worked at ministering who have not become good at it. Experience teaches me that when we launch out with God, we discover that Jesus' promise that we would do what he did and more (Jn 14:12) no longer has to be explained away.

You qualify for this ministry if you have a personal relationship with Jesus Christ, one that gives you the privilege of asking for and receiving the empowerment of the Holy Spirit (Lk 11:13). With that empowerment, all it takes is to launch out in risky faith to practice using the authority and power Jesus has given you.

As you launch out, you need to learn as much as possible of what God has taught others. Read books (see the bibliography), listen to tapes, study the Scriptures, and attend seminars. *But don't seek technique. Seek Jesus—to know him better, to listen to him more closely and to join in carrying out his mission to "bring liberty to the captives" (Lk 4:18).* Join a deliverance team. If none is nearby, form your own with others who will practice and learn with you.

In deliverance ministry, you will experience two precious things. First, you'll be driven to greater intimacy with Jesus as you do what he alone can empower you to do. Second, you will experience renewal as you get healed of your own garbage, develop an incredible thirst for worship and prayer, and become more like the Christian you're meant to be.

MYTH 10: INNER VOICES AND PERSONALITY SWITCHING: SURE EVIDENCES OF DEMONIZATION?

In ministering healing and deliverance, we need to continually remind ourselves that not every problem is demonic. We know this, but it is easy to forget, especially if the symptoms are exceptional—for example, when the person reports hearing voices inside or sometimes seems completely under the control of something angry and hateful. While it is true that demons can be responsible for such voices and personality change, certain psychological conditions also could be the explanation.

The most frequent is probably Multiple Personality Disorder (MPD), defined as "The existence within an individual of two or more distinct personalities, each of which is dominant at a particular time" (American Psychiatric Association, 1980). Those in a deliverance ministry need to learn to distinguish between demonization and MPD for reasons that will become more obvious as we move along.

Not only can alternate personalities talk and behave in ways similar to demons, they are often developed in circumstances similar to those that allow demons to enter. Though I have worked with less than ten MPDs, I have yet to meet a person with MPD who is not also demonized. But even when both MPD and demonization are present, they are not the same thing and need to be treated differently.

A personality is quite different from a demon and needs to be treated accordingly. Integration and healing can be hindered if attempts are made to cast out a personality, on the mistaken assumption that it is a demon. One personality who had been treated as a demon exclaimed irately, "Everybody treats me as if I am a demon. I am *not* a demon! I'm a person!" And she was right—she is a person. But there were demons in her (and in the other personalities inhabiting her body) who sought to block integrating that personality with her core person. They also worked hard to keep all the personalities at odds with each other.

But it's easy to be fooled. For example, both demons and alternative personalities can speak in internal voices. They both can cause physical distress such as headaches, dizziness, and facial distortions. They both can express a range of emotions such as anger, fear, and resentment, though "alters" can express positive emotions more regularly than demons can.

Both alters and demons can exhibit differences in personality characteristics, though an alter can show a greater range of them. For example, I have met demons who whine or plead or who are arrogant, proud, angry, or fearful. Though their arrogance sometimes changed to fear and pleading as they were bested, none showed as wide a range of personality characteristics as the alters I have met. A three-year-old alter I have worked with, for example, though very limited in life experience, exhibits much more personality than the demons of death and fear we cast out of her. So does the seven-year-old alter (living in the same body as the other alter) who had never been out of her hospital bed until Jesus freed her.

For insight into MPD that is both Christian and cognizant of spiritual warfare, I highly recommend *Uncovering the Mystery of MPD* by Dr. James Friesen. He explains the phenomenon in detail and demonstrates the close relationship between MPD and satanic ritual abuse. Startlingly, 97 percent of MPD patients have suffered severe childhood abuse. Furthermore, he estimates that possibly over 50 percent of those with MPD in North America have been subjected to satanic ritual abuse. He shows there is a high probability that children who suffer severe abuse creatively produce another personality to enable them to survive the ordeal.

Friesen's observations have much relevance for our ministry. Those who have undergone severe childhood abuse or satanic and occultic ritual abuse, usually become demonized, and the chance of developing MPD is also a strong possibility. It is, however, important to recognize that treatment for demonization and multiple personalities is different. Indeed, Friesen warns, an alter accused of being a demon could become frightened and become buried within the person for years.[6]

So inner voices and switching of personalities are not always evidence of demonization, though both need to be taken seriously and dealt with in the love and power of Jesus. Though this reality complicates our approach, we can proceed with a minimum of fear if we inform ourselves. As you read on and learn more about demonization, I suggest you also read *Uncovering the Mystery of MPD* and other resource material. Healing people should never be a case of doing it "my way" or not at all. We should always be willing to work with or make referrals to Christian psychologists experienced in areas we do not know well, such as MPD. We need to have a humble attitude, realizing that we are not "the answer" to every problem. Forming a partnership with a good Christian therapist can be an excellent step toward helping those who hurt.

MYTH 11: DELIVERANCE ALWAYS ENTAILS A BIG FIGHT

Two of those who have worked closely with me, Fred and Susie Heminger, had a very unfortunate experience in one of their first encounters A young man they were praying for was violently thrown about by demons for several hours before finally being freed. This helped them come to believe in demons but made them very leery of participating in another bout with one.

Fred and Susie were delighted to learn in one of my seminars that deliverance does not have to include violence. They learned that they have the authority in Christ to forbid violence to happen and now are extremely effective in delivering the oppressed in a calm, loving manner.

Sensational stories of knock-down, drag-out fighting with demons have created the myth that the Enemy is so strong, every deliverance is a battle. Media presentations (for example, *The Exorcist*) and church testimonies also tend to focus on the sensational. "Great physical strength" is sometimes on diagnostic lists designed to help discern whether a demon is present. And we all probably have heard of the need for five burly men to hold down one ninety-pound woman because of the strength of the demon(s) in her!

The belief in such demonic strength needs to be countered. It keeps people from getting into a deliverance ministry, or pushes them out if they have tried it. One pastor told me he turned away from deliverance after a lady threw up all over his office. Now that he realizes that doesn't have to happen, he is once more delivering people. Also, many people who suspect they have demons refrain from seeking help because they fear the battle they think is coming.

It is true that many who have attempted or sought deliverance have found themselves in violent situations. The Enemy loves to use this tactic with people who don't know what they are doing. When demons are approached in the name of Jesus, they become desperate and will try any strategy they think will work to escape. They know their power is nowhere near as great as that of Jesus, so they resort to bluff. As a demon recently said to me, "Ooooh, I'm in trouble now!" They know that many people believe the myth of inevitable violence and they try to exploit their ignorance. If they think they can get away with it, they will stage violence, cause vomiting, arouse fear, and use any diversionary tactic they can think of. You might too, if you were as desperate as they are!

In the heat of the contest, demons will do whatever they are allowed to do. But the key is *what they are allowed to do.* In the name of Jesus, we have power over them. They know this. We need to know it too. They can, therefore, do only what Jesus allows them to do. When we forbid them to cause violence, they can do little or none. We discover, as did the disciples, that when we minister in Jesus' name, "Lord, even the demons submit to us in your name" (Lk 10:17, NIV). They simply exercised the authority Jesus had given them and were able to rejoice in experiencing God's power to banish demons.

People often expect violence because they have believed myths five or six, that the *only* problem is the demons. They have, therefore, fought them at their strongest. They assumed that the demons were the major problem and tackled them head-on, assuming that when the demons were gone, the person would be well. Had they recognized that the real problem was the garbage and worked on it before challenging the demons, they would have found the demons had been weakened and had little or no fight left.

Those who know how to deal with emotional and spiritual garbage first, experience little if any violence. Though some of my colleagues have occasionally experienced violent reactions, *to date in over two hundred cases, I have not had one instance of physical violence.* I believe there are at least four reasons for this:

1. I work almost exclusively with Christians. This means they are indwelt by the Holy Spirit, who assists with the process. If I am asked to work with a non-Christian, I attempt to lead the person to Jesus before working with him or her.
2. Second, I will work only with persons who are willing and eager to be healed. The human will is honored by both God and Satan. It is, therefore, virtually impossible to free someone who does not strongly choose to start and continue, no matter how difficult the process may become.
3. Third, I start each session by forbidding any demons to cause violence or vomiting.
4. Fourth, as I've already pointed out, I do whatever possible to weaken the demons before challenging them. Weak demons often can hardly talk, much less create a ruckus! So they are much easier to deal with than when they were strong.

MYTH 12: THE DEMONIZED SPEAK IN A DIFFERENT VOICE

The roots of this myth are similar to those of the last. There have been situations where, for example, a man's voice came out of a young girl's mouth. Cases like these have led to the belief that a demonized person will *always* speak in a different voice. This characteristic is sometimes on diagnostic lists. Again, we have to thank movies like *The Exorcist* and spectacular stories by Christians for such stereotypes of how demons behave. Many conclude that if the troubled person does not speak in a low, scary voice and have great, uncontrollable strength, demons are not the problem.

As with all these myths, the Enemy delights that large numbers believe this lie as well. Demons are bluffers, who like to frighten people by using other voices. But in the vast majority of cases, demons speak through the natural, or nearly natural, voice of the person they inhabit. Or they simply speak to the person's mind. In this case, the person needs to report to the leader of the ministry team what the demons are saying.

Sometimes a demon will use another language. On one occasion I dealt with a demon in the daughter of a missionary that would speak only Mandarin Chinese. Fortunately, the woman was able to understand most of what the demon was saying. On another occasion, I encountered a demon that would speak only German. In fact, it used some words and phrases that the young woman in whom it was living did not understand. She had to call her husband to interpret the words coming out of her own mouth! In both of these cases, I commanded the demons to speak English, but to no avail, for reasons I don't understand. However, since they did understand what I was saying in English, and knew how to respond to the power of Jesus, both soon were gone.

Many demons seem to be bilingual. I have ministered to a number of Taiwanese and Mandarin-speaking Chinese people. As with the two demons mentioned above, I have often found it possible to speak to the demon in English and received its response in Taiwanese or Mandarin. On one occasion, however, the Taiwanese woman in whom the demon lived spoke quite broken English. The demon, however, spoke much better English than the woman herself did!

My theory with regard to demons speaking in different voices or languages is that factors such as the following either alone or in combination, may enable them to behave in this way.

1. Demons with a stronger grip on a person may use an alternate voice, or another language, or have greater strength, either all the time or on occasion. This is especially true of persons who don't know Christ, thus enabling demons to inhabit their spirit. (I suspect deliverance ministers who work more with non-Christians than I do see this phenomenon often.) I once ministered to a Christian in the strong grip of a demon who used Spanish, German, and English. The demon's host knew neither Spanish nor German!

2. Demons may use this tactic to fool their host into thinking that they are the reincarnation of someone who has died.

3. Demons with particular personality characteristics or a particular assignment from their demonic leaders may use a voice in keeping with their personality or assignment.

HAVE NO FEAR!

For the Spirit that God has given us does not make us timid; instead, his Spirit fills us with power, love, and self-control. 2 Tm 1:7

"Do not be afraid—I am with you! I am your God—let nothing terrify you! I will make you strong and help you; I will protect you and save you." Is 41:10

It is appropriate to end this chapter with a word against fear. The second pastor mentioned in the story at the beginning, was so fearful of the subject of demons that he said he'd "rather not know" if demons were around. The good news is that during our seminar, he learned to not fear demons because he discovered he didn't have to. A bit of knowledge about who he is (a child of God) and how to work with the Holy Spirit to fight demons, changed his attitude greatly. It can change yours also if you are afraid.

Many of us desperately want to respond by "fight not flight," but we fear the battle. To make our problem worse, many of us are ashamed to be afraid. It should come as no surprise to us that both the fear and the shame come straight from the Enemy, the father of lies! One of his chief strategies is to make Christians afraid of him and demonic attack. He likes Christians to be frightened by media images of his amazing power and evil.

Actually, demons are mostly bluff! The power and authority we have in Jesus is *infinitely* greater than the Enemy's. We need to remember that Jesus completely defeated Satan on the cross. As we enter the battle in Jesus' name, then, we have no reason to fear.

Those who watch us minister continually are amazed to see how calmly we can work. They often say, in effect, "I can't believe it. I've always pictured deliverance as scary, with demons exhibiting great power and evil." Knowing how much power is available to us, we simply take control and forbid them to cause problems. Though they may be able to cause a bit of a ruckus, there is really no contest.

THREE

Demonization in Christians

AS EVANGELICALS, we are committed to accepting whatever the Bible asserts. But understanding precisely what it says is often difficult. For example, for years Murphy and I (see chapter one) believed that the following biblical verse and several others proved that Christians could not be demonized: "But you belong to God, my children, and have defeated the false prophets, because the Spirit who is in you is more powerful than the spirit in those who belong to the world" (1 Jn 4:4).

I believe this Scripture. And I wish with all my heart that my earlier interpretation of it were right, that Christians cannot be demonized. But experience has shown me that the verse cannot mean that the presence of the Holy Spirit within Christians makes it impossible for dark angels to live in them. The process by which I free persons from demons proves the truth of this verse over and over, but I have had to reconsider my first interpretation of it.

Demonization came close to Murphy. It also came close to Merrill Unger, a professor at Dallas Theological Seminary whose speciality was demonology. In spite of the fact they both believed it could not happen, a member of each one's immediate family became demonized. These experiences forced them to reexamine the presuppositions underlying their interpretation of such scriptural verses.

Though Scripture is true, our interpretations of it are based on assumptions and presuppositions we carry in our minds when we read the text. *Such assumptions, and the pictures of reality they represent, are known as* "paradigms." A large number of such paradigms or perceptions of reality fit together in our minds to form our worldview. See Kraft, *Christianity with Power* for more on this subject.

When Murphy, Unger, and I looked at what actually happens in demonization, we experienced a "paradigm shift." That is, we changed certain of the assumptions with which we perceived or pictured reality. Murphy calls this particular paradigm shift, or change of assumptions, "the most significant worldview shift in my Christian life."

ANGELA: NOT CRAZY, BUT DEMONIZED

Angela is a Sunday School teacher at a large church in the midwest. She is the mother of two beautiful young children and has been a Christian since she was sixteen years old. Angela loves Jesus.

We met Angela following a spiritual warfare seminar. Angela was desperate. Since early childhood, she had been fighting against what she called "evil powers." As a child, she would wake up every night and feel evil spirits trying to touch her. After she became a Christian, these experiences seemed to subside, although she still encountered them some nights. However, the past two years had been "worse than ever before." The "evil powers" were waking her in the night, closing in on her, and telling her to do terrible things to her family.

Angela had been in counseling with a Christian therapist for two years. She had received much support from that counsellor, as well as from her pastor, church friends, and loving family. None of them, however, raised the possibility of demonic influence. Even with all their help, she couldn't get rid of the troubling voices and fears. After hearing the conference teaching on Christians and demonization, though, she came to us in tears. "Until now," Angela cried, "I thought I was crazy. I had given up hope. Now I know it's not just me, that these evil powers are demons. For the first time in years, I have hope that I can get well."

Angela was right. During a ministry session, the Holy Spirit clearly revealed that she was demonized. Angela was wonderfully delivered of the demonic spirits that had been troubling her since childhood. Jesus also healed her of the emotional wounds to which the spirits were attached. Her life was changed, and she is now ministering the love and healing of Jesus to others in her church.

Ministering to people like Angela is a privilege and a joy. Her love for Jesus, like that of Mary Magdalene out of whom Jesus had cast seven demons (Lk 8:2), is an inspiration. An important reason for sharing her story is that it is typical of many to whom I have ministered. The vast majority of demonized Christians are, like Angela, devoted to Christ, but either don't realize demons exist or don't believe that demons can live in Christians.

CAN DEMONS LIVE IN CHRISTIANS?

The discussion over whether Christians can have demons living within them stems from two sources: the terms that are used and the lack of experience within the Christian community in delivering people from demons.

As we saw in myth two, the concept of "demon possession" has gained credibility through a poor translation of Greek terms referring to people who have demons living within them. If "possession" is to be used at all, it should label only those who are so totally controlled by demons that their whole being is taken over by the alien personality from time to time. I have never met, and only rarely heard of a Christian for whom "possessed" could even be considered appropriate.

The deliverance ministries of my acquaintance, however, all agree that Christians can have demons living within them. Dickason (*Demon Possession and the Christian*) treats the subject exhaustively. He states, "I have encountered from 1974 to 1987 at least 400 cases of those who were genuine Christians who were also demonized... I would not claim infallible judgment, but I know the marks of a Christian and the marks of a demonized person. I might have been wrong in a case or so, but I cannot conceive that I would be wrong in more than 400 cases."[1]

The story of Merrill Unger, author of several books on demonology (*Biblical Demonology, Demons in the World Today, What Demons Can Do to Saints*), is instructive. In his classic, *Biblical Demonology,* he took the position that only unbelievers could be demonized. He then received many letters from around the world disagreeing with him. These, plus an experience in his own family convinced him to take a new look at the Scriptures. He realized that his position "was *inferred,* since Scripture does not clearly settle the question. It was based on the *assumption* that an evil spirit could not indwell the redeemed body together with the Holy Spirit (emphasis mine)."[2]

The discovery, painstakingly detailed by Dickason,[3] that *the Scriptures give no support to the theory that demons cannot live in the regenerate,* led Unger to reverse his position. As Dickason points out, the question of whether Christians can have demons is like asking whether Christians can have cancer. He exhaustively examined every Scripture reference that could relate to the issue and found none to prove conclusively either that Christians can or cannot be demonized. Without a clear scriptural position, then, we need to consult those with experience in dealing with the problem under consideration.

Those who work with cancer patients know that Christians

can and do develop cancer. Likewise, those with "clinical" experience with Christians having demonic symptoms have overcome their doubts and concluded that Christians can and regularly do carry demons. They also have discovered that the power of Christ can break the demons' power and banish them from the believers in whom they have been trespassing.

As one example among many, I have been working with a young woman I'll call Jennifer. She has been an active, committed Christian for several years, but had heard voices in her head for as long as she could remember. These voices specialized in putting her down and contradicting any pleasant or positive thought about life and herself. They regularly tried to dissuade her from worshiping, Scripture reading (in fact, they affected her eyes to hinder this), witnessing, or seeking help. They steadfastly and strongly criticized her to keep her self-concept low, attempting to convince her she could not do many ordinary things.

We found out from the demons behind Jennifer's voices that they had entered her before she made a commitment to Christ and that they had tried hard to keep her from becoming a believer. Failing that, their task became to keep her from experiencing all that Jesus could offer her. They admitted they had lost her spirit and that Jesus now lived there. They didn't like that one bit but were doing their best to diminish her life.

One evening as we ministered to Jennifer in the power of Jesus, we challenged the demons behind the voices and cast them out. She no longer hears the voices and can now enjoy worship and preaching in a totally new way. Most other things in her life are also brand new as well, and Jennifer ministers regularly to others to bring them the freedom she now experiences (2 Cor 1:4).

With over two hundred such cases in my own experience, over four hundred in Dickason's (see *Demon Possession and the*

Christian), the "conversions" of Unger and Murphy and the concurrence of every expert I know of who has actually worked with demonized people (for example, Koch, *Occult Bondage and Deliverance*; Bubeck, *The Adversary*; Murphy, *Spiritual Warfare*; White, *The Believer's Guide to Spiritual Warfare*), the evidence that Christians can be (and frequently are) demonized is so conclusive that we can be dogmatic about asserting it. So, as Dickason writes, "The burden of proof lies with those who deny that Christians can be demonized. They must adduce clinical evidence that clearly eliminates any possibility in any case, past or present, that a believer can have a demon... we must note that those who deny that Christians can be demonized generally are those who have not had counseling experience with the demonized. Their stance is largely theoretical."[4]

As in Jennifer's case, demons in Christians are usually left over from their non-Christian past. I have, however, dealt with many demons that have been allowed in by Christians during lapses in their Christian lives—for example, Carolyn Murphy.

One significant fact, often not pointed out by those who write on demonization, is that "demons cannot indwell a Christian in the same sense that the Holy Spirit indwells. God's Spirit enters a believer at salvation, permanently, never to leave (Jn 14:16). A demon, by contrast, enters as a squatter and an intruder, and is subject to momentary eviction. A demon never rightfully or permanently indwells a saint, as the Holy Spirit does."[5]

The way the Holy Spirit enters is, I believe, by uniting with the spirit, "heart," or innermost being of the person who surrenders self to God. I have tested this scores of times, as I did with the demons in Jennifer, by commanding demons (under the power of the Holy Spirit who forces them to be truthful) to tell me if they live in the person's spirit. They consistently reply something like, "No, I can't get in there. Jesus lives there." When they are commanded to tell when they had to leave the Christian's spirit, they give the exact date of the person's conversion.

I conclude, therefore, that demons cannot live in that innermost part of Christians, their spirit, since it is joined to and filled with the Holy Spirit (Rom 8:16). That part of Christians becomes alive with the life of Christ and is inviolable by representatives of the Enemy. *Demons can, however, live in a Christian's mind, emotions, body, and will.* Deliverance ministries regularly kick them out of those parts of Christians. I suspect it is because demons can invade even the spirits of unbelievers that they can have greater control of them.

In conclusion, many of God's people are suffering from demons, and it is imperative that we fellow Christians learn how to help them. As believers attempting to demonstrate the compassion of Jesus, we can no more turn them away than we turn away the poor and hungry.

SALVATION AND DEMONIZATION

When people give their lives to Jesus and become Christians, a miracle takes place. Jesus Christ himself comes to live inside them. A transfer of power and ownership is made. Those who once belonged to the "ruler of this world" (Jn 14:30) now belong to Jesus, and it is he who rules in their lives. All has become new (2 Cor 5:17) in the deepest part of their being—their spirit. The central and most important part of each person, the part that died when Adam sinned (Gn 2:17), is now made alive and becomes the home of Jesus.

Jesus, the new ruler, rescues them from the kingdom of the Enemy and places them in the kingdom of God. Our Lord won the right to do this by defeating Satan at the resurrection. From the moment people decide to give their lives to Jesus, the one who lives within them is greater than the former ruler, the one who is in the world (1 Jn 4:4).

But, as we all know, new believers still have a lot of work to do to achieve the goal of becoming "conformed to the image of [Jesus]" (Rom 8:29, NKJV). They must still contend with their old sin nature. For reasons we do not understand, our sin nature is not eradicated when we accept Christ. We must fight for every inch of sanctification. But with the Holy Spirit within us to help us, we can make great progress.

We see the same scenario with regard to demonization. The vast majority of demonized Christians are demonized when they come to Christ. They have experienced a change of rulers in their spirit, but they have not attained complete freedom. A demonized person, like Israel, has been given "the land" but still needs to conquer it.

All who come to Christ have the sin nature to conquer. The demonized person who comes to Jesus, however, has both the sinful human nature and one or more demons to conquer. And the two are related, as we will see.

HOW DEMONIZATION HAPPENS

To understand how demonization occurs in a Christian, we need to understand how demonization happens to anyone, Christian or not. For, as noted, most demonized believers became so before their conversions.

Demons can gain entrance in several ways:

1. Demons can enter by invitation. A five-year-old boy I'll call Jerry ran and hid behind a couch to escape the blows his father was aiming at him. As he did so, he silently cried out "Help!" He immediately felt comforted. From that time on, whenever he was beaten by his father or mistreated by anyone, all he had to do was to call and the same comfort would come. As I worked with Jerry, now thirty-five years old, we discovered that his comforter was in fact a demon. Though he still often comforted Jerry whenever asked, he was also doing destructive things in Jerry's life.

A young woman I'll call Amy, felt angry over her helplessness, and began searching for power by reading occult books and listening to satanic rock music. She soon found she could "make things happen" by wishing them. Amy was on the high school softball team but was not on the first team. Another girl was better in softball than Amy. When Amy wanted to play, however, all she had to do was "wish" the other girl sick, and it happened.

Teresa, though a Christian, became discouraged when some promises made to her were not kept. We already had cast scores of demons out of her, so she knew the freedom Jesus can bring. Nevertheless, in her discouragement, she invited in a spirit named Protector, who apparently had been living nearby for some time, just waiting for such an invitation.

These cases, plus that of Carolyn Murphy cited earlier, illustrate that demons can enter when asked. To get a better concept of how common such invitations must be, add to these examples the New Age practice of seeking "spirit guides"; the conscious invitations given to demons in satanic rituals; the common non-Western shamanistic rituals (designed to get people "possessed" or "mounted" by demonic spirits), plus what must be an incredible number of private invitations to demons.

People differ, however, in their awareness of what they are doing when they invite demons in. Teresa, for example, was quite conscious that she was asking for demonic assistance. She had experienced the presence of more than a hundred demons—demons that are now gone and forbidden to return. She knew what demonization was. But undoubtedly helped by demonic tempters, she deluded herself into thinking her discouragement would be overcome by calling for Protector. Before it was cast out she had had a protector spirit and now sought the kind of encouragement she remembered having received from that spirit, even though she knew all he could offer was counterfeit encouragement.

Carolyn, Jerry, and probably also Amy, however, were not nearly so conscious of what they were asking for. Carolyn seemed to drift into the decisions that allowed the demons in. Jerry simply called out into space. And Amy, though she deliberately sought power, probably had no idea of its source and of the dangers to which she was exposing herself. In fact, when I asked her if she would like to be delivered from the clutches of the demon(s), she refused. "I'm enjoying the power they give me," she said.

A major problem for these people, as for the rest of us Westerners, is our ignorance of the spiritual world. We have been carefully taught that demons are okay in fairy tales but that they don't exist in reality. The "reaching out" for power and the experimenting with rock music that exalts Satan and demons are not, therefore, seen for what they are—*very dangerous.*

Laws and principles in the spiritual realm are every bit as binding as those that operate in the physical realm. Even an unconscious invitation for demons to enter has the same effect as an unconscious breaking of the law of gravity. If we stumble, no matter how unconsciously, we fall because we are subject to the law of gravity. Or if we consciously declare that we don't believe in the law of gravity and defy it, we soon find we are subject to it whether we want to be or not. The same is true of spiritual laws. *Invite a demon, consciously or unconsciously, and you get a demon, whether or not you know what you are doing or even believe in demons.*

Dealing with potentially demonized Christians means, among other things, looking into their backgrounds for any indication of either conscious or unconscious invitations for the Enemy's emissaries to enter. Things to look for include:

Conscious invitation of demonization is probable whenever there has been deliberate involvement with or worship of gods/powers other than the true God. Few, if any, of those involved in satanism or witchcraft escape demonization since they consciously open themselves up to invasion. Likewise, those involved in the occult aspects of the New Age movement. Though such practices as seeking spirit guides and channeling are clearly demonic, not every aspect of New Age is occult. Even many of the more innocent looking activities, however (such as those related to health and the environment), put the participants in great danger of becoming demonized. Other occult involvements to look for include organizations such as Freemasonry, Christian Science, and Scientology. Attending séances, going to fortune tellers, being involved in "table tilting" and levitation are also occult. Even more innocent-looking activities such as playing with ouija boards and tarot cards put a person in great danger.

We classify these activities as *conscious* invitations in spite of the fact that persons in our society, given our worldview blindness to the spirit world, often do not know they are inviting demons. Few involved in Freemasonry know, for example, the risk in which they are putting themselves and their families. Yet the decision to participate in these functions is a conscious one, just as a decision to defy the law of gravity is conscious, whether or not one knows the law.

Unconscious invitation differs in that it is more subtle. This kind frequently occurs when one "wallows" in a negative attitude resulting from a difficult past experience. For example, a person who is being physically or emotionally mistreated is reacting normally by getting angry. When, however, the anger is clung to, causing permanent resentment, bitterness, and unforgiveness, a weakness is created that can give the Enemy opportunity to enter the person. Such attitudes create what I call emotional or spiritual "garbage" that demons can feed on.

Demons cannot enter and stay without a "legal" right. They gain this right when we do not get rid of normal, yet potentially harmful, reactions such as anger. The anger itself is not a sin. We read in Ephesians 4:26, "*If* you become angry. ..." The implication is clearly that we will become angry. But when that happens, we are told to "not let your anger lead you into sin, and do not stay angry all day." The reason for this admonition, then, is given in the next verse, "Don't give the Devil a chance" (Eph 4:27). And a few verses later we are further told, "Get rid of all bitterness, passion, and anger. No more shouting or insults, no more hateful feelings of any sort. Instead, be kind and tender-hearted to one another, and forgive one another, as God has forgiven you through Christ" (Eph 4:31-32). Jesus strongly emphasizes the need to forgive. Right after the Lord's Prayer, he tells us, "If you forgive others the wrongs they have done to you, your Father in heaven will also forgive you. But if you do not forgive others, then your Father will not forgive the wrongs you have done" (Mt 6:14-15).

Wallowing in unconfessed sin (for example, sexual sins, misuse of power, pledging supreme allegiance to someone or something other than the true God) is another common unconcious invitation to demons. So is repeatedly giving in to potentially addictive behavior (for example, pornography, drugs, lustful thoughts, envy, worry, fear, and self-hate). Repeatedly, I find that demonized people are holding onto one or more such weaknesses and refusing to confess and deal with them as sins. This failure undermines their spiritual defenses, providing what John Wimber has pictured in a lecture as "a runway with lights showing the way for demons to enter."

We need to make an important point here. Though all of these attitudes and behaviors, whether sinful or not, are very dangerous, they do not automatically result in demonization. Some apparently have higher resistance than others. However, the more one wallows in such dangerous attitudes and behavior, the greater the risk of unconscious demonic infestation. Demons study human beings and are quick to take advantage of any opportunity to get inside.

To avoid such danger, we need to deal both with obvious sins and with any suspicious attitudes and behavior. We are responsible to God to work with him on the "garbage" in us, the works of our human nature. Such works cannot be cast out. "What human nature does is quite plain. It shows itself in immoral, filthy, and indecent actions; in worship of idols and witchcraft. People become enemies and they fight; they become jealous, angry, and ambitious. They separate into parties and groups; they are envious, get drunk, have orgies, and do other things like these" (Gal 5:19-21; cf Col 3:5-9).

The Enemy actively encourages all such behavior and frequently finds entrance through the weaknesses they cause. Scripture is clear that whether or not there is demonization, these sins must be dealt with by repentance and self-discipline. And Scripture implies no demonization for some of the greatest sinners it mentions (for example, the adulteresses of Jn 8 and Lk 7, or the sinful Corinthians of 1 Cor 5-6).

Demons cannot enter, then, simply because a person commits a sin. They can, however, enter if a person chooses *not* to repent or to resolve any given sin and consequently wallows in it. Continuance in sinful attitudes creates opportunity for demonization. Sins of the flesh need to be repented of and resolved before they become demonic "runways."

The good news is that we can work in the power of the Holy Spirit, both to deal with any sin or attitude or behavior, and to banish any demons that may be attached to them. How this can be done will become clearer as we move along.

2. Persons can be demonized through the invitation of someone in authority over them. A woman I'll call Tricia was brought up in a satanist family. Her mother, in accordance with her satanic faith, dedicated Tricia to Satan. At that point one or more demons entered Tricia, having been invited by one in authority over her. Such dedication of children to spirits or gods is a common practice worldwide.

On a few occasions I have ministered to persons who were conceived after their mothers sought spirit power to become pregnant. This resulted in their being demonized from the moment of their conception. The mother of a Taiwanese woman had undergone a Buddhist temple ritual prescribed by its priest. In another case, the mother of an American woman had consulted a fortune teller.

Adults who submit to cult leaders can become demonized

through dedication or satanically empowered "blessings." Parents can demonize their children through cursing (see point four below). Cursing can also result in demonization of wives by husbands and vice versa.

3. Demonization through inheritance. I cannot understand why God allows this, but children may become demonized through heredity. We often refer to this as the passing on of *generational or "bloodline" spirits/power.*

Sometimes one or more spirits are inherited. I have frequently found this to be the case with people whose parents and/or grandparents were in Freemasonry. This is not surprising since Freemasons regularly curse themselves through the secret oaths they take. In the higher degrees, they dedicate themselves and their families to Lucifer (see Shaw and McKenney, *The Deadly Deception*).

At other times, apparently what was inherited was not a demon but a weakness or "hook" that allowed a demon to attach itself. Not infrequently, I have discovered that a given demon is rooted in inheritance from both father and mother. Recently I uncovered a spirit of rage, inherited from both father and mother. If the man had inherited a spirit of rage from each parent, I'd expect to find two spirits of rage. But he had only one. Perhaps he had inherited two but one left. Or perhaps he inherited a propensity, much like the tendency to acquire certain diseases. Demonization happened, then, as soon as a demon came along that was able to take advantage of the propensity—to "grab the hook" provided by the inherited weakness. Either way, the man was demonized and the roots were in his inheritance, rather than in his choice or that of someone in authority over him.

Spirits that are passed down through the generations within a family are often called "family" or "familiar" spirits. Typically, they have gained entrance through the commitment of or curse put on an ancestor. Such generational spirits tend to cause similar emotional problems, sins, illnesses, or compulsions from generation to generation. Suspect a generational spirit if you see both in someone being ministered to and in past generations of that person's family, such problems as alcoholism, depression, sexual perversion, hyper-criticism, extreme fearfulness, cancer, diabetes, or almost any other emotional or physical problem or besetting sin. We discovered that one woman's grandmother, her mother, and she herself had needed hysterectomies in almost the same year of their lives. Though this did not prove the existence of a generational spirit, it alerted us to look for one, and we found it. *Since most of the symptoms we deal with in deliverance ministry can be the result of any of several different causes, we must not jump to conclusions quickly.*

4. Demons enter through cursing. We have mentioned cursing several times already. Cursing is very common and I have frequently found a curse to be a major factor in the power a demon has over a person. But *cursing does not always result in demonization.* Indeed, demonization that occurs solely as the result of cursing is probably rare. Cursing and its siblings—dedication, oath making, the casting of spells, and hexes—however, often combine with other factors to bring about demonization.

The above-mentioned weaknesses or misuse of authority probably would also need to be present for a curse to enable a demon to enter. I suspect that if a person does not have some such inner weakness or if that person is protected through intercessory prayer, a curse would simply "bounce off" without being able to enter. Perhaps that is what Proverbs 26:2 means. In two translations this verse says, "Curses cannot hurt you unless you deserve them. They are like birds that fly by and never light" (Today's English Version). And, "Like a fluttering sparrow or a darting swallow, an undeserved curse does not come to rest" (NIV).

A curse is the invocation of the power of Satan or of God to affect negatively the person or thing at which the curse is directed. The invo-

cation may be through words or thing(s) that have been cursed or dedicated. The words used may be as mild as "I hate..." or "You'll never amount to anything," said to others or to oneself. Or they may be more forceful: "I wish... were dead" or "May... never succeed in..." or "God damn you" or "I curse you with ..." The power of the curse may be increased through the use of a ritual. In addition, cursed or dedicated objects in a person's possession can provide enemy forces the opportunity to afflict the person, even if not demonized (for example, Carolyn Murphy, whose story was related in chapter one).

Scriptural examples of curses empowered by God are those directed against the serpent (Gn 3:14), the ground (Gn 3:17-19), Cain (Gn 4:11-12), those guilty of certain sins (Dt 27:15-26; 28:15-68), those cheating God (Mal 1:14; 2:2; 3:9), whoever hangs on a tree (Dt 21:23; Gal 3:13), those who ridiculed Elisha (2 Kgs 2:23-24), anyone who rebuilds Jericho (Jos 6:26), and a fig tree (Mt 21:18-19). As Christians we have God's power to back up curses. We must be careful with our words lest we be invoking that power wrongly. We are to bless, not to curse (Rom 12:14; cf Lk 6:28).

As mentioned earlier, demons seem to be able to "hook onto" curses that have been leveled at a person's forbears. A prominent Christian leader converted from a Jewish family once described for me the total newness that came into his life when he was delivered from a demon hooked onto the curse the Jewish people put on themselves at the time of Jesus' crucifixion: "Let the responsibility for his death ("his blood," NIV) fall on us and on our children!" (Mt 27:25). In a woman with a French background I found a spirit of arrogance connected to a curse of (or dedication to) French cultural pride. We once worked with a woman whose ancestry included seven generations of handicapped women. After the curse was broken and the woman was freed of the demon, she gave birth to a healthy baby girl.

However access is gained by demons, let me point out again that the vast majority of the demonized Christians I have ministered to brought their demons with them into Christianity. Though it is certainly possible for Christians to become demonized, I have dealt with few whose infestation was not connected to pre-Christian attitudes and behavior.

WHAT FREEING PEOPLE FROM DEMONS ENTAILS

Early in my experience in prayer ministry, I learned some important basics. These apply to all prayer ministry, including deliverance. I strongly recommend them:

1. Our subject is people, not demons, technique, or even healing. It is *people* God loves. It is *people* God wants to free. It is *people* over whom the battle is fought between God and Satan. Our job is to minister to *people*.

2. Our object: To free people at the deepest level. Our mandate, like that of Jesus (Lk 4:18-19), is to free prisoners from whatever problems the Enemy is utilizing to hurt and harass them. If this is simply a physical problem, that is all we deal with. Usually, though, a physical problem is tied to something deeper, often in the emotional area. Our task is to discover the deeper problem and claim the power of the Holy Spirit to bring to it whatever healing God desires to bring.

3. People are tightly interconnected. Our Western compartmentalized approach to healing isn't working. People with physical problems consult physicians and often are not healed because the underlying malady is not treated. People go to psychologists for emotional difficulties and often are not healed because spiritual factors are overlooked. If we are to work effectively with God for complete healing, we need to take a comprehensive approach to those who hurt.

4. Never assume the problem is simply physical, emotional, spiritual, or demonic. Most of the people we minister to are suffering in several, if not all, these areas. A client may complain of a splitting headache plus other physical problems, but soon reveal that she hates herself, is angry and bitter toward her parents and husband (emotional problems), feels deeply guilty over certain things in her life, and is unforgiving toward those who have hurt her (spiritual problems). She may, in addition, be living under the influence of demons of death, hate, rejection, guilt, control, and many more.

5. If there are demons, they are attached to something inside the person. Demons cannot live in a person without something to "feed" on. Something always will be in the person that gives the demons a "right" to be there. *Demons are like rats, and rats go for garbage.* Demons usually attach themselves to emotional or spiritual problems. Getting a demonized person well, therefore, means dealing primarily with the emotional or spiritual "garbage," and only secondarily with getting the demons out. We find that most people who attempt deliverance ministry don't realize this, especially at the start. They tend to focus on getting rid of the demons as soon as possible. If they get the demons out without healing the emotional or spiritual hurts, however, chances are high that the demons will return. They can legally reclaim their right to feed on the garbage, since it is still there. When we get demons out, we want them to stay out, so we try to make sure the garbage is gone too.

Dealing with demons will, therefore, be treated here as a subcategory of what many call "inner healing," or what I like to call "deep-level healing."

FOUR

Our Power and Authority

DO WE KNOW WHO WE ARE?

When I was a youngster, my dad was a part-time policeman in addition to his full-time job. Of course, he wore a uniform. Sometimes he took my younger brother and me places while wearing that uniform. Whenever we were with him, we got special privileges. I remember when I was about seven or eight, he took us to the town fair. Because Dad wore a uniform, we didn't have to pay to get in! As we went to the ice cream stand, I heard, "Good afternoon, Mr. Kraft. How are you today? Oh are these your boys?" Dad would introduce us proudly. "Yes, this is Charlie, and this is Bobby."

The next words were "Would you boys like ice cream cones?" We gave the expected answer, of course. Again, Dad did not have to pay—for the cones or for any of the other "goodies" we were given! Being with Dad when he wore that uniform made us feel really special. We were given privileges no one else was given. It was neat to be the son of a policeman!

There was, however, a problem for me. I didn't feel that my dad paid much attention to me otherwise. I didn't understand that times were tough—that if he didn't put in lots of hours at work and find ways to shore up his own self-image, we wouldn't survive. All I knew was that I felt neglected and unable to relate to this father whom I admired so much. This made me feel worthless and driven to achieve in order to attract his attention and, hopefully, his admiration.

These feelings grew into anger at myself and self-rejection. I didn't like my looks, my mind, my emotions, my name ("Charlie"). I felt I was "unlucky" and developed a terrible temper—rooted, probably, in my anger toward myself and my situation. I even tried to run away from home, feeling that no one at home cared anyway. I wished continually that I could be someone else.

Even after accepting Christ at age twelve, my struggle continued. I was happy to be headed for heaven but terribly disappointed that I wasn't experiencing more of the newness promised in 2 Corinthians 5:17. The same habits persisted, the same self-hate, the same desire to be someone else, the same inability to talk to my dad or other authority figures. I still considered myself unlucky. Other people seemed to be having more good things happening to them than I did. I felt like Charlie Brown, "If anything goes right for me, it must be a mistake!"

I readily assimilated and identified with what I read and heard preached concerning human sinfulness. That made sense to me. What I couldn't relate to were verses of Scripture telling how special each person is to God. Such verses had to be for someone else. I didn't know, and wouldn't let myself hear, who I really was and am in God's eyes. When I became aware of such truths, I would often argue with God, saying such things as, "If you really knew me, you wouldn't accept me like that." I simply could not accept God's opinion of me!.

What God says, though, is:

Consider the incredible love that the Father has shown us in allowing us to be called "children of God"—and that is not just what we are called, but what we *are.* 1 Jn 3:1, Phillips

For all who are led by the Spirit of God are sons of God. And so we should not be like cringing, fearful slaves, but we should behave like God's very own children, adopted into the bosom of his family, and calling to him, "Father, Father." For his Holy Spirit speaks to us deep in our hearts, and tells us that we really are God's children. And since we are his children, we will share his treasures—for all God gives to his Son Jesus is now ours too. **Rom 8:14-17, LB**

And because we are his sons God has sent the Spirit of his Son into our hearts, so now we can rightly speak of God as our dear Father. Now we are no longer slaves, but God's own sons. And since we are his sons, everything he has belongs to us, for that is the way God planned. **Gal 4:6-7, LB**

These verses assure us we are *special* to God. For me, it has taken a long time to accept this as truth and to stop arguing with God about who I am. His word and his behavior toward us can, however, be trusted. So now I like to ask discouraged Christians, "Do you know who you really are?" People usually answer such things as "a Christian," "a believer," and "redeemed." Those answers are, of course, true. And each is precious. But, to me, the most precious of all the claims we can make about our relationship with God is that he has adopted us as his *children*, his own sons and daughters.

We are fashioned in God's image—something that cannot be said of any other being. Then, when we fell, God redeemed us, forgave us, and replaced our sin nature so that "God's very nature is in [us]; and because God is [our] Father, [we] cannot continue to sin" (1 Jn 3:9).

This position endows us, then, with both the authority and the inheritance that belong to members of God's family. *Think of it, we have been adopted right into the family of the King of the whole universe!* He wears a special uniform and has privileges wherever he goes—and we, his children, get to share in all those privileges.

SATAN DOESN'T LIKE THIS AT ALL!

Our Enemy is opposed to our discovering who we are. Indeed, he is greatly threatened by us and the position God has given us. And, since his primary concern is to enhance his own position in the universe, it is to be expected that he is jealous of us. For we (not he) are in second place in the universe. Only we (not he nor any other creature) are created in God's image. And, though both Satan and humans rebelled, only humans have been redeemed from their rebellion. Was redemption offered to Satan and his followers? We do not know. If it was, Satan's kingdom has rejected it.

What we do know, though, is that any human being who trusts Jesus Christ is restored to the relationship with God for which we were created. We again become members of God's family. This makes our Enemy jealous and anxious to do all he can to keep believers from discovering who they really are. He, of course, doesn't want us to discover who God is. But *he is equally afraid we'll discover who we are.* He is jealous of the attention God showers on his children and the position he gives them. Satanic beings counter by spying out our weaknesses and exploiting them to the fullest, especially in areas where God has given us something they don't possess.

He especially targets the godlike characteristics that God has built into us. For example, only we are in God's image. So he works hard to cripple our self-image. Only we and God can create new beings who are in God's image. So Satan attacks our sexuality. Only we and God can relate to others at a deep spiritual level. So he attacks human relationships, especially between family members, but also any other close relationships that are vulnerable.

In his jealousy that God has redeemed humans, Satan attempts to darken people's minds to keep them from responding to the good news of God's redemption (2 Cor 4:4). If he is successful, he can continue to live in the spirits of the people he has deluded. This is the condition God called death in Genesis 2:17 when God said, "If you eat the fruit of the tree, you will die." If, however, people give themselves to Jesus, Jesus comes to live in the person's spirit, evicting any demons and preventing, or at least severely reducing, Enemy activity there.

But Satan does not give up. He continues to do whatever he can to keep God's people from fully entering into the riches of their inheritance. As in my own experience, the Enemy loves to get us to connect feelings of rejection with a sense of our own sinfulness, so that we reject, ignore, or argue against God's acceptance of us. Satan's dark angels are, of course, actively trying to get us to sin. If we follow their promptings and fall, then, they don't let up even after we have confessed the sin. Their job at that stage is to keep us from feeling forgiven. For, if they can keep us from accepting God's forgiveness, we will be so loaded down with guilt that we'll not function well.

The Enemy apparently is able to put thoughts in our minds —especially doubts concerning our status with God, and the reasonableness of how he deals with us. How often we hear "Forgiveness can't be that easy," or "That's not fair of God," and "Who do you think you are, to think God will forgive you after what you've done?" Satan is the author of "worm theology," in which we see ourselves, even after we are saved, as worms ("for such a worm as I").

We have found Satan particularly active in the emotional area. Perhaps this is related to our culture, since our society is especially hard on people emotionally. I think, however, that human emotions everywhere are particularly susceptible to satanic attack, since the harboring of negative emotions so easily leads to sin. When, for example, a person is hurt, the natural reaction is anger. But if the person does not get rid of that anger, it turns into sin. So we are commanded in Ephesians 4:26-27 to get rid of it before that point: "If you become angry, do not let your anger lead you into sin, and do not stay angry all day. Don't give the Devil a chance." We are, likewise, to "get rid of all bitterness, rage and anger, brawling and slander, along with every form of malice," showing, rather, kindness and compassion "to one another, forgiving each other, just as in Christ God forgave you" (Eph 4:31-32, NIV). In addition, we are warned not to allow ourselves to wallow in fear (Is 41:10 and many other passages), worry (Phil 4:6), lust (Mt 5:28), and other negative emotions.

The Enemy has good reasons and diverse tactics to keep us from discovering who we are and how we should behave toward him. He knows that *with the Holy Spirit in us, we have infinitely more power than he does.* The question is, do we know who we are and how God has empowered us to wage the battle?

If we are children of the king of heaven and earth, we are certainly a lot more than either our society or our churches usually make us out to be! Many of us simply don't believe down deep inside that we have anything like the status God gives us. Low self-esteem, poor father images, and countless insecurities keep us from realizing the incredible inheritance our Father has given us. As a part of this inheritance, we get to judge angels someday (1 Cor 6:3) and to cast some dark ones out of people right here and now.

Children of a king are called *princes and princesses.* And so we are. Every Christian is a prince or princess of the most high king, Jesus. Do we, then, walk with our heads down? Royalty does not walk that way, even in Enemy territory. Our Father owns this earth, even though it is temporarily under the rule of a trespasser (1 Jn 5:19). We can, therefore, walk with our heads held high, knowing who we are and who our Father is.

IF ONLY WE KNEW HOW MUCH POWER WE POSSESS!

If only we Christians knew how much power we possess! A friend of mine was chatting with a woman who recently had been converted to Christianity out of the occult. While serving Satan, she had the ability to "see" the amount of spiritual power people carry with them. According to her, every person carries a certain amount of spiritual power, but the difference in power between Christians and non-Christians is amazing. Indeed, she could spot Christians immediately in any group, even at a great distance, by noting the amount of spiritual power they carried. She now knows that the reason for this difference is the presence of the Holy Spirit in them.

She remarked, though, that she and her occult group felt no threat from most Christians, even though they knew Christians were more powerful than they were. For the Christians had no idea how to use the power within them. Though that power (that is the Holy Spirit, the source of their power) afforded them much protection from evil power, they did not know how to use the Holy Spirit's power to go on the offensive in spiritual warfare.

The occult group discovered, however, that some Christians did know how to use their power. The servants of Satan learned to steer clear of them, for they could be a threat. Fortune tellers, occultic healers, and others working under the power of Satan discover, for example, that when Christians are around, they cannot operate smoothly. A missionary friend of mine once went into a Mexican cathedral where several *curanderos* (occultic healers) were at work. He simply sat down and prayed against one of them. As he sat there praying, the healer looked up at him several times, then packed up her paraphernalia and left with her client. The missionary's praying had canceled her ability to carry out her functions. *How different things would be for a lot of Christians if only they realized how much power they carry.*

Such stories certainly stretch the worldview of Western Christians. But they are true. The question, then, is how does the fact we Christians carry incredible spiritual authority affect our lives and ministry? The Bible has a lot to say about spiritual authority. Let's take a closer look at the Scriptures to better understand where we as Christians stand in this regard.

SPIRITUAL AUTHORITY

Jesus called the twelve disciples together and gave them power and authority to drive out all demons and to cure diseases. Then he sent them out to preach the Kingdom of God and to heal the sick. Lk 9:1-2

Jesus drew near and said to them, "I have been given all authority in heaven and on earth. Go, then, to all peoples everywhere and make them my disciples: baptize them in the name of the Father, the Son, and the Holy Spirit, and teach them to *obey everything I have commanded you.* And I will be with you always, to the end of the age." Mt 28:18-20, emphasis mine

Anyone who has faith in me will do what I have been doing. He will do even greater things than these, because I am going to the Father. Jn 14:12, NIV

Studying the Gospels reveals that Jesus not only spoke about the kingdom of God but demonstrated that it was already present on earth. As he indicated, the fact that he drove out demons "proves that the Kingdom of God has already come to you" (Lk 11:20). Jesus repeatedly made clear that he operated with God-anointed spiritual authority. Over half of the Gospel of Mark is devoted to Jesus' demonstrations of this authority through healing and deliverance.

Jesus made it plain, however, that he didn't limit this authority to himself. During his earthly ministry, he conferred on his apostles (Lk 9) and the seventy-two (Lk 10) the "power and authority to drive out all demons and to cure diseases" (Lk 9:1). With this authority and power, they were to heal the sick and let people know that "the Kingdom of God has come near you" (Lk 10:9). Jesus intended that his followers imitate his approach to witness, accompanying words with power (see Acts 1:8).

From Jesus' words in Matthew 28:20, we learn that he meant for his followers to teach their followers what he had taught them. They were to teach their followers "to *obey everything I have commanded you.*" That this teaching was to include performing signs and wonders seems clear from his promise in John 14:12 that we will be able to do what he did, and more!

I have struggled with the issue of spiritual authority. After all, who am I to think I can do the works of Jesus? I fully believed I was much too sinful and ungifted to believe what I've just written. (I wonder where that thought came from?) My mentor, however, simply said, "Try it and see what happens." What happened was that I (and each of those who sat with me under John Wimber's teaching early in 1982) discovered that *when we assumed that Jesus was talking to us and launched out to "do the works," amazing things happened.*

The more I studied the Scriptures from this point of view and the more I experienced, the more I became convinced that Jesus meant for us to exercise the same spiritual authority he gave the disciples. And for the same purposes. Jesus came to defeat Satan both during his life and through the cross and resurrection. Time and time again, we see him exercise his spiritual authority over the Enemy in Scripture. Then he says to the disciples and us, "As the Father sent me, so I send you" (Jn 20:21), and with the specific promise that anyone who has faith in him will do what he did and even greater things (Jn 14:12).

STUMBLING BLOCKS FOR PRINCES AND PRINCESSES

I pray that you will begin to understand how incredibly great his power is to help those who believe him. It is that same mighty power that raised Christ from the dead and seated him in the place of honor at God's right hand in heaven. **Eph 1:19-20, LB**

We are God's precious children—princes and princesses in his kingdom. As we have just learned, part of our inheritance as his children is incredibly great power, the *same* power that raised Christ from the dead. This power within each of God's children is greater than that of the entire satanic kingdom.

Why, then, do so many of us Christians have trouble believing in the spiritual authority God has given us? And why do we go even further and question that we are God's precious children? Many of you are probably struggling this very minute with what I am saying about your inheritance and authority as God's child. You would like to believe that you are a prince or princess but deep within, you wonder if that is really true. *It is.* The Enemy, however, is committed to keeping you from knowing who you are and the authority and power that is yours because of who you are.

As a result of my own struggles to accept who I am in Christ, I began teaching my Sunday School class on the subject. I used a book I strongly recommend to all who fight feelings of inadequacy and low self-worth. It is Neil Anderson's, *Victory over the Darkness.* Several members of my class spoke of exciting changes in their lives as they worked through the biblical truths Anderson presents in his book.

Let me assure you of the truth that as a Christian, you are God's precious child and an heir of his power and authority. Some stumbling blocks may be in your path, as they were in mine. Let me discuss some common ones and what to do about them.

1. You may not be experiencing the freedom of Christ. It is difficult to appropriate the riches of our inheritance in Christ, including the authority and power he has given us, unless we are experiencing his freedom in our own lives. As Paul says, "Freedom is what we have—Christ has set us free!" (Gal 5:1). The fact is, however, that many Christians are not free. We may have given our lives to Christ and even been used by him in ministry, but inside we find that living and working for Jesus involves a constant fight with problems that never seem to go away completely.

They are probably emotional wounds—what I call "garbage" —resulting from your reactions to the hurts you have experienced, often during childhood and the teenage years. When we are hurt, we react—often with anger, resentment, fear, or similar negative emotions. These are not inappropriate reactions, given the fact that someone has done or said something that hurts us. The problem arises, however, when we hang onto these emotions and "wallow" in them. Jesus doesn't deny our right to our feelings. He himself showed anger on several occasions. But he did not let these emotions lead him into sin. Rather, he gave them to the Father before sundown, lest he give the devil a chance (Eph 4:26, 27) to find something by means of which to gain a "hold on" him (Jn 14:30, NIV).

Unfortunately, many of us have not learned what I refer to (please pardon the analogy) as the law of "spiritual excretion." In our physical bodies, we have an excretory system. It sees to it that material that cannot be used or could hurt us, is regularly eliminated. If for some reason that system gets blocked or doesn't function properly, we get poisoned from inside. The same seems to be true in the spiritual and emotional realms, except that we have to control our spiritual and emotional excretion by acts of our will. This process doesn't take place as automatically as the physical one does.

Just as we feel a sense of relief after physical elimination, we feel at peace or rested after spiritual excretion. The process involves simply giving up our *right* to anger, bitterness, revenge, and like emotions, and giving our feelings to Jesus. By so doing, we allow him to carry our impossibly heavy burdens and to repay any who needs to be repaid (Rom 12:17-21). This is, I believe, what Jesus is referring to when he says, "Come to me, all of you who are tired from carrying heavy loads, and I will give you rest. Take my yoke and put it on you, and learn from me, because I am gentle and humble in spirit; and you will find rest. For the yoke I will give you is easy, and the load I will put on you is light" (Mt 11:28-30).

The stakes are high both for you and for the plans God has for you. If you let the Enemy continue to have a hold on you (Jn 14:30), you are, in effect, a *prisoner of war* in the cosmic battle between God's kingdom and that of Satan. You have been disarmed so that your weapons will do you no good. Neither will the authority and power that Jesus has given you. You are locked up in a prison without knowing that Jesus has made it possible for you to be released and set free from those things Satan has used to bind you.

The fact that many do not know what freedom feels like has been brought home to me by the reactions of several people just after they were delivered from demons. They remarked that they now felt very strange. Though it is usual for a person to feel free and light, a man I'll call Art exclaimed, "I feel weird!" Art just lounged there on the couch where he had been sitting with a strange look on his face. My thoughts, which he seemed to read, were something like, "Oh no, we've got more work to do." But he interrupted to explain that for more than eighteen years, he hadn't experienced "the feel of freedom" and had even forgotten what it felt like. Now, as freedom flowed over him, he just wanted to sit for awhile and enjoy it. I met Art a couple of years later and learned that "feel of freedom" has never left him.

In a second situation, a missionary I'll call Julie didn't even recognize the feel of freedom. Julie had grown up as the oldest daughter in a family with an alcoholic father. She had, therefore, been forced to take major responsibility in her home from a very early age. In the process, she had become infested with a strong demon of control. When I met her in the country where she and her husband served as missionaries, she had been nearly incapacitated for almost a year with deep depression. When she was finally freed from the strong demon of control and the weaker one of depression (plus several others), it was obvious to her that something had changed. But, since she could not remember ever having felt freedom, she didn't know how to interpret the change. She thought she was back in depression! Some of her co-workers helped Julie to understand, though, and now, over two years later, she is still "flying."

Not everyone who has emotional or spiritual garbage inside them is demonized. But even the problem of demonization is secondary to that of getting rid of the garbage. If, therefore, you have been experiencing a lack of freedom in your emotional or spiritual life, you should seek the kind of ministry we call "inner healing," "prayer counseling," or "healing of the memories." As a part of such ministry, if demons appear they can be flushed out and sent away. And you get to be free!

2. You may have a self-image problem. As mentioned earlier, the Enemy is especially hard on us in the self-image area. Several aspects of Western societies are very helpful to him in this process. Our individualism and competitiveness cut us off from relationships with others. We are taught to define ourselves in comparison to others according to what we do, how we look, how we perceive we are accepted, and how much we have achieved, rather than in terms of who we are. Our normal standards of comparison with others are usually based on such ephemeral things as possessions, physical attractiveness (especially for women), number of (usually superficial) friendships, and how well we have assimilated and can regurgitate what is often irrelevant information.

In all of this, there is great opportunity to discover and focus on those areas where we fall short in comparison to others. Many of us live our days constantly falling short of our standards and feeling we are unacceptable to ourselves, others, and God. We seem neither to know that our standards are unattainable nor that God's standards are quite different.

We really want to believe God loves us. We want to take our place as a "prince" or "princess" in his kingdom. We want to believe in the tremendous power available for us as his children. But our self-condemnation keeps us from accepting what is rightfully our inheritance.

As I've already related, I personally have struggled with this problem. For years, I had a "negative tape" inside my head continually playing the Enemy's lies. He said things like "Reject yourself, you're no good," "You are a no good, failure-prone sinner, and will never be anything else," "Carry your guilt, your sins are too great for even God to forgive," "See how unworthy and inadequate you are, you're always messing things up," "Worry about what others think of you," "Fear that you're going to fail again," and so on. In short, those messages were telling me I was unacceptable and unworthy to be the prince God has adopted me to be.

By opening up to God's truth and utilizing his healing power, however, I am being "reprogrammed" by Jesus and am learning from him to receive his acceptance and love. The "tape" he plays in my mind conveys quite different messages, true messages. He says to me, "Because I have accepted you as you are, you can accept yourself"; "I love and accept you for who you are, not for what you do"; "You are forgiven, you don't need to feel guilty anymore"; "I chose you, don't argue with my choice"; "I have made you worthy and adequate"; "I will never leave you or forsake you"; "Don't fear, cast all your cares on me, for I care for you"; and the like. I'm still trying to sort this all out and to rework my habits. Indeed, as I sit here reminding myself of these truths, I can't hold back the tears of joy (tinged with disbelief) that *the king of the universe thinks enough of me to grant me far more love and acceptance than I ordinarily grant myself.*

He wants you to hear him saying the same things to you. His desire is that you truly understand, deep within, his love for you and your place in his kingdom.

In his book *The Seven Gifts*, Bernard Kelly uses a powerful analogy to help us understand the difficulty Christians have in accepting their inheritance. Kelly likens this struggle to a slum child that was adopted by a royal family. At first, the slum child rejoices that he is out of the slum and living in a palace. The child's new father, the king, tells the slum child that he no longer needs to live in the dark, hateful streets where he once lived. Furthermore, the king tells his new son that all of the royal family treasures now belong to him as their adopted child. In spite of this joyful inheritance, the child remembers the way people in the slum treated him and the abuse he suffered. Something within him cries out, "It can't be true!"

Unfortunately, this poor slum child has brought much "slum baggage" with him to his new palace. The royal family could take him out of the slum, but getting the slum out of him is another matter. Fortunately, his new loving parents understand this, "take his hand," and teach him to trust their unconditional love. Caringly, patiently, they help him along until he can truly acknowledge and accept his new life and inheritance.[1]

Many Christians react exactly like that slum child! They have been given a new life and inheritance as children of the Most High King! Like the slum child, they too bring their baggage of hurts and wounds. We have internal tapes that cry out, "It can't be true!" It is here that we need to give the Holy Spirit our hand, and seek healing of the wounds that block acceptance of our rightful inheritance. Jesus desires that our stumbling blocks—our self-hatred, our low self-esteem, our fears, our unworthiness—be removed. He wants to help us step forward to claim our rightful place as his children.

Inner healing and the freedom that follows are possible through God's powerful ministry to you. If no inner healing ministry is near you, try reading and following guidelines laid down by such authors as Seamands (*Healing for Damaged Emotions, Healing of Memories, Healing Grace*), Sandford (*The Transformation of the Inner Man, Healing the Wounded Spirit*), or by listening to my tapes (see bibliography). In addition, sit quietly before the Holy Spirit and ask him to bring to mind events in which your self-image was damaged. Ask him to let you see Jesus in each event and allow the Lord to minister to you. As he does, accept your true relationship with him and thank him for who you are. Between such intimate times with Jesus, continually affirm for yourself the truths of Scripture concerning who you are, to ward off and overcome the attacks of the Enemy on your mind and emotions.

3. You may not have a proper view of God. As indicated earlier, Satan does not want us to understand who God is and the implications of this truth. The Enemy is especially anxious to keep us from discovering who God wants to be to us. God wants to be our father in the fullest sense of the word, but the meaning we attach to the word "father" is often the biggest roadblock to our letting him become to us all he seeks to be.

When we give ourselves to Christ, we are adopted by a heavenly Father in whose presence we are welcome at any time. We are invited to "approach the throne of grace with fullest confidence, that we may receive mercy for our failures and grace to help in the hour of need" (Heb 4:16, Phillips). Many of us, however, struggle with the reality of a heavenly Father who unconditionally loves and accepts us. The reason may be that we have not experienced such love and acceptance from our earthly fathers. Many of us have endured neglect and even abuse from our fathers, and can't imagine any other kind of treatment from someone called "father."

I have ministered to a number of people whose concept of "father" had been damaged in major ways. One woman's definition of father had become, "Someone who always stands in my way whenever I really want to do something." Another's came out in the statement, "Whenever I picture Jesus, I always see him with a stick in his hand." For still others, "father" may be someone distant and unconcerned or one who has abused them psychologically, physically, or sexually. Such people usually find that at the deepest level they cannot accept the truth that God is not like their earthly father—even though they have accepted that truth on a rational level.

Another problem for many people is their anger at God for allowing bad things to happen to them. They have been taught that God can do anything he wants. When they have experienced difficulty, they reason, it must be because God didn't care enough about them to protect them. So they are angry at God and convinced he endorses their low opinion of themselves.

Such false perceptions of our heavenly Father provide some of the greatest blocks to understanding and functioning in our spiritual authority. Faulty pictures of the Father or of Jesus need to be corrected before we can take our rightful place as God's princes and princesses. We must renounce and refuse to listen any longer to the lies we've been hearing about our Father.

The key to becoming free to understand and relate properly to God the Father is forgiveness. If we are angry at God, we need to "forgive" him. By forgiving God, I mean to stop holding anger and bitterness toward him for allowing things to happen that we feel he should have prevented.[2] We don't understand why he allows people to get hurt, and he usually never explains (he didn't explain to Job). But, since his ways and thoughts are as far above ours as the heavens are above the earth (Is 55:9), we have to give up our attempts to understand God, and simply accept that the God we relate to will do right (Gn 18:25). We then give up our right to be angry at him, committing ourselves to trust him and refusing to dictate how he should run things.

Having "forgiven" God, it is critical that we forgive our earthly father, no matter what he may have done to us, and no matter how often he did it. Again, it is no sin to become angry or even to desire revenge. But if we *assert* our right to them, the harvest is predictable. In the emotional area, as in every other, the law of the harvest (that is, we reap what we sow, Gal 6:7) governs the outcome. Sow the seeds of anger, revenge, bitterness, and hate, and I can promise undesirable fruit such as emotional instability, negativism that ruins relationships, and physical illnesses such as cancer, arthritis, diabetes, and the like. Plus, perhaps, demons to reinforce such problems.

The solution, however, is simple. Just as with sin, we are to acknowledge our emotional attitudes, confess them to God, give them to him, and never take them back. We are then to forgive the guilty person unconditionally, just as completely as God has forgiven us. The rule is, "If you forgive others the wrongs they have done to you, your Father in heaven will also forgive you. But if you do not forgive others, then your Father will not forgive the wrongs you have done" (Mt 6:14-15). And you are imprisoned by your own unforgiveness.

The result of forgiveness—the fruit of sowing forgiveness—is that *both the one forgiven and the one who forgives go free!*

Having forgiven our earthly father, we are free to love him, and thereby come to a new understanding of our heavenly Father.

We need to be careful how we evaluate the behavior of our earthly father (or mother or other relatives) toward us. Most of those who have abused their own children have suffered similar or worse abuse themselves. This does not excuse them. They still are guilty and responsible for their actions. This fact does, however, enable us to understand that their behavior usually was not willful but *driven*. Behind their behavior was not a cool evaluation of what they were doing and a choice that they believed was right. Rather, they were not in control of their behavior but were driven by emotions such as anger, bitterness, and desire for revenge, rooted in their own life experiences and often reinforced by demons. In reality, their outbursts were not aimed at us, but at those in their backgrounds who had hurt them. They are more to be pitied than condemned.

Even fathers who are not abusive often make mistakes, and big ones. Often we fathers have simply capitulated to our own insecurities and feelings of low self-worth at the expense of our children. We may have simply followed the dictates of society that give us "points" for what we do in our career but none for being good fathers. So we have worked hard to be successful in the eyes of our co-workers and others at the expense of our children. If your father was like that, please forgive him for neglecting you. He (and I) need your forgiveness for waking up too late. And recognize that your heavenly Father is not like us. He is never too busy to spend time with you. Indeed, he says, "I will never leave you; I will never abandon you" (Heb 13:5).

If you, like most Christians, have struggled with a wrong or inadequate view of your Father in heaven, Jesus wants to heal you. He wants you to know the depths of his love for you. Your Father wants you to know deep within that you are his precious child. To move in this direction you may find it helpful to pray something like the following:

Dear Jesus,

I truly want to know your love for me. I deeply desire to know what it means to be a prince/princess in your kingdom.

With gratitude for all you have forgiven me, I willingly forgive my earthly father (and everyone else who has hurt me) for everything they have done that has hurt me.

Please heal any blocks within me that prevent me from understanding my inheritance. Please free me from any self-image problems or fear.

Come, Holy Spirit, teach me and lead me into the spiritual authority and power you give to your children. Thank you, Lord, for loving me. Amen.

OUR GREATEST WEAPON—INTIMACY WITH JESUS

"Not by might nor by power, but by my Spirit," says the Lord Almighty. Zec 4:6, NIV

Our greatest weapon in fighting satanic influence—whether in ourselves or in others—is our intimacy with Jesus. Jesus set the example by living his life in constant closeness to the Father. He was listening to the Father at all times. Thus he could say, "I say only what the Father has instructed me to say" (Jn 8:28). He was continually watching what the Father was doing. Thus he could say, "the Son... does only what he sees his Father doing. What the Father does, the Son also does" (Jn 5:19). He lived in absolute dependence on the Father. Thus he could say, "By myself I can do nothing. As I hear from God, I judge, and my judgment is true because I do not live to please myself but to do the will of the Father who sent me" (Jn 5:30, Phillips).

Those were Jesus' day-by-day directives. To be certain his sights were lined up with those of the Father, then, he regularly spent time alone with the Father. Over and over again we read that Jesus withdrew "to a solitary place" (Mt 14:13, NIV) to be alone with the Father.

As we reach out to bring healing and deliverance to those in need, it quickly becomes apparent that we are not the healers. Healing and deliverance don't happen because we are gifted. People are touched, healed, and delivered because God himself is with us. It's important to remember that it isn't by *our* might or power, but by *his* spirit. Cultivating the intimacy with Jesus that enables constant working with and dependence on his spirit is, therefore, the first order of business.

Such intimacy is not the mysterious thing many people make it out to be. It doesn't have to involve religious ritual. People often ask me, "How do you prepare for a deliverance session?" The truth is, I seldom do anything special. Rather, I try to stay prepared constantly, because I never know when I'll be called upon. A good example is the case of the pastor who was delivered in a restaurant, described in the last chapter. The other day I received a telephone call "out of the blue" from someone I had never met. Within half an hour I was interacting with and casting out demons. Whether over the phone or in person, that's often about as much warning as I get. So I try always to be prepared by staying close to Jesus.

Spiritual authority is, I believe, in direct proportion to spiritual intimacy. Our power comes from the indwelling Holy Spirit. Our authority comes from keeping on good terms with our Lord.

FIVE

What Demons Do

MAKING BAD THINGS WORSE

Be alert, be on watch! Your enemy, the Devil, roams around like a roaring lion, looking for someone to devour. 1 Pt 5:8

For when I forgive... I do it in Christ's presence... in order to keep Satan from getting the upper hand over us; for we know what his plans are. 2 Cor 2:10-11

People often ask me if I believe all the bad things in life are caused by demons. The answer is, No. A similar question is, "Is everybody with recurring emotional or physical problems demonized?" The answer is again, No. Then they ask me, "How can we tell the difference?" The answer to this question is more complicated.

Let's review some basic understandings of the spiritual conflict between God and Satan: (1) There is a kingdom headed by Satan and populated by a very large number of demonic associates; (2) These beings are out to disrupt God's workings as much as possible; (3) They are especially concerned to hurt God's favorite creatures—humans—the only ones God made in his own image; but (4) Satan and his followers can work only within the rules God has laid down for them.

99

We know Satan cannot do anything without God's permission. He seems, however, to have permission to do quite a lot. But there also seems to be a rule that says he cannot influence a person without a legal right. He can only take advantage of a right that is already there, he cannot cause anything without what is often called an "entry point." Another way of saying this is, though he can piggyback on something already there, he cannot cause difficulty unless something is already there for him to "build on."

With this as a basic rule, then, the Enemy sets himself to latch onto bad things to see if he can't make them worse, and to push people to go overboard with good things, to throw things out of balance. He looks, therefore, for both weaknesses and strengths to exploit, but he exploits each in different ways. And he knows things about us that we may not be aware of.

I was once asked to give a series of talks for a group of charismatic pastors and their wives. As I stood up for my second talk, I felt an insistent pain in the left side of my lower back. Though we paused for a group of the pastors to pray over me, I could not go on and had to leave the platform. In a more private setting, another of the pastors prayed over me and within an hour, I passed a kidney stone and was able to return to the group to finish my talk.

Though I had never had kidney stone problems before, the Enemy knew one had formed and chose the time of my talk to take advantage of that weakness. I later had a similar experience while I was in the middle of getting several demons out of a missionary. Between sessions, the big toe on my right foot got very sore. During the next session, one of the demons said through her, "I got your toe!" He had found a weakness there and exploited it. It did him no good, however. We kicked him out anyway.

How do we know whether it's the Enemy or not? I believe at least two points can be made in response: (1) Since the members of the satanic kingdom are out to do whatever damage they can to human beings, I think we can assume that whatever problem arises, they will be there to exploit it, and (2) Since satanic beings can only take advantage of conditions already there, we need to look for such conditions and deal with them. We cannot simply claim, with Flip Wilson, "The Devil made me do it."

The Scriptures always hold us responsible, even if Satan is involved. Peter was responsible for the words that came out of his mouth when he rebuked Jesus (Mt 16:22-23) and later denied him (Mt 26:69-75), even though the Enemy was clearly involved. Apparently, there were weaknesses in Peter (insecurity? fear? doubt?) that the Enemy was able to take advantage of on those occasions to get him to do his bidding.

If we are to be effective in ministering to the demonized, it's important to recognize the typical ways in which the members of Satan's kingdom go about their work. Paul could assume that the Corinthians knew the Enemy's schemes (2 Cor 2:11). Unfortunately, the worldview blindness of most Westerners means that we have to be much more explicit in our day. Our people simply do not have the awareness that the scriptural writers had and that God expects us to have. The Enemy does indeed prowl around "like a roaring lion" (1 Pt 5:8). He seldom roars, however, unless he is noticed. He is intelligent enough to work largely in secret among those who don't believe (or barely believe) he exists.

When we become aware of demonic workings, though, the representatives of the Enemy are usually not too hard to spot. They are very predictable, not particularly creative, and often repeat the same tricks. One way to develop "spiritual eyes to see" demons is to study common ways they attack. We need to do this if the Enemy is not to outwit us. After all, what good soldier goes into battle without first understanding the way his enemy operates? Let's, therefore, take a closer look at the common tricks demons pull, so we can become better equipped to fight them.

THINGS DEMONS ENCOURAGE

Let's begin by looking at several kinds of activity demons encourage—either from outside or inside those they attach to (including all who read this). I consider it very likely that each of us has at least one demon assigned to work from outside us to spy out our weaknesses and exploit them. It is probable, then, that those who are the greatest threat to the Enemy have more or stronger demons assigned to them.

Demons seek to get into people. Presumably, they will have more opportunity to influence from inside. If they cannot get in, however, they work from outside as best they can. In the list that follows, I will not distinguish whether the Enemy's forces are working from inside or outside. My aim is simply to point to the kinds of things they seek to do from whatever position they can achieve.

1. We can assume that demons are involved in every kind of disruption. I am careful not to use the word "cause," since I believe their ability to initiate problems is very limited, if possible at all. Rather, they push, prod, tempt, and entice to get people to make bad or at least unwise decisions. And, when they find someone already in difficulty, they work to make it worse. If God were not actively protecting Christians and non-Christians alike, the accidents, fractured relationships, abuse (physical, mental and sexual), and disruption we would experience defy imagination.

As we have noted, Christians are special targets of the Enemy. Rita Cabezas, a psychologist friend of mine discovered this fact right from a demon's mouth. Her session with a demonized Christian woman was being observed by a non-Christian psychologist who asked the demon why he lived in the Christian woman rather than in him, the non-Christian. The reply was, "You are of no interest to me. You already belong to the evil one.... Evil is within you—deeply rooted." The demon even gave the names of four of the demons living within the man. But, referring to the demonized Christian, the demon said, "I'm interested in getting *her*. We are interested in possessing *her and* [pointing to two other Christian women] *her and her.*" Earlier the demon had said, "I am interested in destroying, in tormenting her so she doesn't pray, doesn't seek God, so that she will fall away from him and be like the rest of them.... I'm in her mind. Not within her but in her mind" (Cabezas, *Des Enmascarado*).

The aim of Satan's servants is to cripple and destroy as much of God's work as possible, whether it's happening through Christians or non-Christians. They, therefore, zero in on individuals, groups, organizations, ministries, and governments, whether sacred or secular. They seek to produce strongholds (2 Cor 10:4) where their strength is greater, perhaps because there are more of them or because their tentacles are hooked more deeply into the person or group.

2. Demons are probably the primary agents of temptation. It was probably demons doing Satan's bidding who tempted Cain (Gn 4:4-8); Noah and Ham (Gn 9:21-22); Sarah and Abraham (Gn 16:1-3); Shechem (Gn 34:1-2); Tamar and Judah (Gn 38:12-26); Joseph (Gn 39:7-10); and a host of others in Scripture including Peter (Mt 16:22-23; 26:69-75); Judas (Lk 22:3-6); and Ananias (Acts 5:3).

Demons apparently can put thoughts in our minds, though, again, we are responsible for what we do with those thoughts. Since demons know what each of us is susceptible to, they will tailor the thoughts they put in our minds, so they will be appropriate for each person. For example, demons seldom tempt a person in the sexual area who is not already vulnerable in that area. Nor are they likely to tempt a non-religious person to go overboard in the religious area, or one unconcerned about money to become a miser. Or a younger person with something appropriate to an older person, or a man with something appropriate to a woman.

They constantly hammer away, however, and will do whatever it takes to tempt, in hopes that they can contribute to the person's failure. That is their job.

3. Demons seek to keep people ignorant of their presence and activities. This strategy is particularly effective in Western societies. Demons like people to be ignorant of their presence and love it when people don't believe they exist. Demons have repeatedly referred to this strategy during ministry sessions. During a recent session observed by a psychologist learning about demonization, a demon became so angry it yelled, "I hate it that she [the psychologist] is learning about us. For years, we've been hiding and making them think we are psychological problems!"

The fact that demons piggyback on problems already in the person rather than originating problems enables them to hide quite effectively. If people can explain the problem as resulting from "natural" causes, they may see no need to look further. Often, however, the function of the demon is to reinforce the problem in such a way that the person gets discouraged and stops fighting it. And the Enemy the person never suspected was there gets a victory. Frequently people say to me, "I thought I just had to live with that problem," or "Since I knew the problem was generated by my dysfunctional family background, I thought there was no hope." And many do give up hope, thinking they are crazy or that nothing can be done about it.

Demons delight in working behind the scenes, pushing people to react in dysfunctional ways and then encouraging them to blame themselves. Often I've ministered to people with spirits of fear that tried desperately to get the persons to fear me. Others have had spirits of deceit that pushed them to tell me lies. Some have had violent spirits that tried to get them to be violent with me. These people have been amazed to learn that their responses were not simply their "natural" reactions. They had, over the years, gotten so used to such reactions they thought they were completely their own.

4. Another demonic tactic is to get people to fear them. If they can't keep people ignorant, often their next strategy is to work on people's fear of what they don't understand or what they see as potentially embarrassing. In this regard, many of the stories told of dramatic deliverance experiences play right into the Enemy's hands.

The fear tactics demons employ take many forms. I've ministered to people who feared they had a demon. This led them to assume something must be very wrong with them spiritually. They didn't realize that the presence or absence of a demon usually has little to do with one's present spiritual condition, except to hinder it. Many of my clients have been very mature spiritually, in spite of the impediments caused by the spirits inside of them. The people I've dealt with have more often become demonized through inheritance, some kind of abuse, or pre-Christian involvement, than through spiritual failure and rebellion. Often, then, the demons in such persons have become very weak because of their spiritual growth. I have heard demons express consternation countless times over their inability to get a stronger grip on some persons because they are "too close to Jesus."

By contrast, people come for ministry who are afraid they don't have a demon! They often would like to avoid responsibility for their problems and are hoping to blame them on demons. These clients may be difficult to work with because they resist taking responsibility for dealing with the underlying garbage that gives demons a toehold in their lives. Others, however, have been told they must be crazy or permanently disabled, so they genuinely hope that a major part of their problem is demonic and, therefore, can be corrected. It usually can.

Many people fear the power of demons. They have heard stories, seen movies, or talked to people who got involved in physical battles with demonized people. I have already mentioned the pastor who gave up dealing with demonized people when one threw up all over his office. When he learned that such a problem can be avoided simply by forbidding the demon(s) to do it, he was willing to begin again. Most of the physical battles can be avoided in the same way—command the demons to stop! The real contest is not a physical one, anyway. It is spiritual and won through the use of empowered words, not muscles.

When one realizes how little power the Enemy has compared to that of God, very little fear should remain. We should never take the Enemy lightly, but most of what looks like power on his part is deceit or bluff, or both. *He really has little more than the power given him by the person he's in.* If, then, that person's will is engaged against the demon(s), it is only a matter of time until the demon(s) have to go. Though a struggle may take place until the person's will is on God's side, as soon as the will has been given to God, the tough part is over. And most people who come for deliverance prayer already have chosen to turn to God for help.

5. In all satanic activity, deceit is a major weapon. Satan is called by Jesus, "the father of all lies" (Jn 8:44). Since lying "is natural to him," he continually lies to anyone who will listen. He lies about who we are, he lies about who God is, he lies about who he is and what he does. As in Eden, he deceives through direct contradiction ("That's not true; you will not die," Gn 3:4) but, perhaps more often, through indirect questioning, as when he asked Adam and Eve, "Did God really tell you...?" (Gn 3:1). Who of us have not heard questions like these in our minds: "Would a just God allow that to happen?" or "If he cared about you, would he have let you be born to these parents?" or "Can I really be forgiven this easily?" or "Am I really saved?" or...

They illustrate a favorite trick of the Enemy: Deluding people that such false ideas are their own. One thing I like to do during deliverance sessions is to force demons to state some of the lies they have been telling. Clients are usually amazed to discover the source of much of their negative thinking (usually about themselves, others and God) that has been keeping them in captivity. One woman, after hearing the demon report about twenty-five falsehoods, exclaimed, "I've been hearing every one of those lies several times a day for all of my life!"

6. The job of demons is to hinder good by any possible means. Demons try to keep people from God or from doing anything God wants. They hinder unbelievers from believing (2 Cor 4:4). They also work to undermine the faith of Christians. Worship, prayer, Bible study, expressions of love, and acts of compassion are high on the demonic hit list.

But the basic demonic strategy is to discover and attack weaknesses. Demons don't play fair! The greater the weakness, the more often a person is likely to be attacked in that area. They are like vicious predators who, smelling blood, keep after wounded victims until they can do them in. Failing a kill, though, they will settle for the maximum possible amount of hindering.

7. Demons, like Satan, are accusers. Dark angels regularly expose people to accusations of every kind. Many of these are perceived negative attitudes of others toward a person. A common tactic is to convince people to accuse themselves, others, and God of causing whatever may be undermining their health, life, love, relationships, and anything else that comes from God.

The self-rejection engendered by Western societies provides especially fertile ground for satanic accusations. I can't count the number of people I've prayed with whose major problem was their own inability to accept themselves. One of them, asked why she felt she needed prayer ministry, simply said, "I hate myself!" Demons like to piggyback on such negative attitudes to get the person mired in self-accusation.

They also like to plant thoughts that lead us to accuse others, including God. Demons encourage rumors, cultivate misunderstandings, and justify anger at and blame of God.

Satan nags people into retaining guilt even after they have confessed sin and been forgiven by God, convincing them something is incurably wrong with them. He persuades people to blame themselves for abuse they have received from others. More, he strongly suggests that troubles are from God and deserved because of one's failures. He's skillful, too, at leading people to blame others for difficulties they themselves have caused. Among satanic whispers about God are: "He's not fair," or "He can't be a good God if he let's bad things happen," or "His forgiveness doesn't come that easily."

Accusations directed against oneself, once accepted, often lead a person into self-cursing or vows against themselves that the Enemy gladly empowers. Many who fall into self-rejection find themselves saying such things as: "I hate my body (or my face or my sexual organs or my personality or some other part of myself)," or "I wish I were someone else," or "I will never be like (or I will be like) so and so," or "If I can't measure up to such and such a standard, I would rather die." Such statements constitute curses and vows that must be renounced in the power of Jesus Christ if they are not to result in damage to the person making them.

Western society's standards for the female body frequently are used by demons to get women to hate and curse their bodies or any part of them they believe doesn't measure up to the ideal. Those who have been sexually abused often believe the Enemy's lie that it was their fault, leading them to curse their sexual organs or even their gender. They are often enticed into statements such as, "I hate (or resent or reject) such-and-such parts of my body," or "I hate being female."

A woman I'll call Jill came to me distraught over the discovery of lumps in her breasts. As I asked God what to say and do, the word "abuse" came to me. I asked Jill if she had ever been sexually abused. "Yes," she said and indicated that her breasts had been the focus of the man's interest. "Have you cursed your breasts?"

"Yes," she said, "many times, by strongly wishing I didn't have them for men to be interested in." She renounced the curses and the next week the doctor could find no lumps!

Accusations by the Enemy are a major factor in many manifestations of self-rejection.

8. Demons reinforce compulsions. Demons delight in helping people develop compulsions toward both good and bad behavior. A pastor's wife I'll call Dianne described her husband, Al, as compulsive in everything he did. Whether working, studying, making love, or ministering, she said, Al went about it compulsively. One day while Al sat in one of my classes, a fairly strong demon made its presence obvious to him. We were able to deliver Al from the demon after class. Three weeks later, during a seminar I was leading, Dianne stood before the group to exclaim, "I've been living with a different man this last three weeks! The compulsiveness is gone."

Demons, of course, reinforce such compulsions as lust, drugs, alcohol, tobacco, overeating, undereating, pornography, gambling, materialism, competitiveness, and the need to be in control. What is not so obvious is that they also encourage exaggerated attention to many things ordinarily considered "good." Among such compulsions are work, study, attractive dress, religion, doctrinal purity, family, achievement, and success.

The usual demonic approach to compulsion is to build on people's weaknesses and exaggerate their strengths. Compulsions often are rooted in fear, insecurity, and feelings of worthlessness. Demons are quick to exploit these attitudes to make the person compulsive.

9. Harassment: another demonic tool. A major concern of the Enemy is to disrupt people's lives, especially those of Christians. He nips at our heels like an angry dog whose space has been encroached on. Satan is referred to as "the ruler of this world" (Jn 14:30), and doesn't like it that those who belong to another King are wandering around in "his" territory, so he harasses Christians whenever and however he can.

I don't know how much power demons have over the ordinary circumstances of life. But I would wager that they do whatever God allows to disrupt our lives through influencing such things as traffic, weather, health, stress, relationships, worship, sleep, diet, and machines (especially cars and computers). I suspect, for example, that harassment was the aim of Satan when he ordered demons to manifest when Jesus was teaching in the synagogue (Lk 4:33-4), that it was he who stirred up a storm while Jesus was in a boat on Lake Galilee (Lk 8:23-4), and that he influenced the Pharisees to persecute Jesus continually. I have developed the habit of saying when things go wrong, "If this is the Enemy, stop it!" It is amazing how many difficulties fade at that command.

Demons like to influence churches and their congregations. How often have you found your mind wandering during the sermon? Or had a hard time getting into worship? Or didn't feel up to par? Or seen, heard, or thought of something that broke your concentration just at the wrong moment? Or had a fight in the car on the way to church? Demons also like to influence pastors to run churches as clubs rather than as hospitals, to focus on preaching and program rather than ministering to people, to preach theoretically rather than practically, to perform rather than to communicate. They push musicians to show off, those who give announcements to interrupt the flow of worship, and ushers to be too obvious. In short, their goal is to weaken what God wants to do through the church. Harassing Christians is a primary assignment of demons. Learning the Enemy's schemes (2 Cor 2:11) makes us aware of this fact and challenges us to learn how to counter Satan's activities.

But Satan doesn't seem to harass every Christian equally. He seems to pay more attention to those who are the greatest threat to him and to those who don't have enough prayer support. Many Christians are so passive about their Christianity that they are no threat to the Enemy. They may get off with very little attention from him. I even heard of a pastor who made a bargain with Satan that he would not preach against him if he didn't cause disruption in the pastor's ministry! His was certainly a "wood, hay, and stubble" (1 Cor 3:12, Phillips) ministry, destined to be destroyed when tested by fire. How much better to be such a threat to the Enemy that he feels it worthwhile to attack us. How much better to hear our Master say to us someday, "Well done" (Lk 19:17).

Those who threaten the Enemy and do not have enough prayer support also are at risk of regular and effective harassment. It is wise for us to get a number of people supporting us in prayer, especially those with gifts of intercession, before we move strongly against the Enemy. We will then take territory from him and frustrate him because we will have too much prayer protection for his attacks to get through. The fact that even Jesus was harassed and that weak Christians seem to be, suggests, however, that no Christian lives completely free from the Enemy's attention as long as they are in his territory.

The tactics listed above apply to demonic activity whether coming from outside or inside a person. Predictably, satanic beings usually can attack with more intensity and effectiveness if they are working from inside. There is, however, good news: even if we have demons living inside us, our continuing growth in Christ can diminish their ability to affect us. Furthermore, if we deal with the emotional and spiritual garbage inside us through counseling or prayer ministry, the grip of the demons can be reduced dramatically, even before they are cast out.

The remainder of this book will deal with how demons behave when they live inside. I will not, therefore, develop this topic further at this point.

MORE OBVIOUS DEMONIC ACTIVITY

Sometimes demons act in more obvious ways. This happens when they are bold, when they are foolish, and when they are forced by the Holy Spirit to let their presence be known.

1. Evil spirits may become bold for tactical reasons. Perhaps demons believe that they can harass more effectively through becoming more obvious. They may assume that the person they are afflicting will "freak out" when confronted by a "presence," especially when that person is alone and in the dark.

Boldness or confidence seems to be behind the appearance of demons as dark presences that people can see or feel, usually at night. Such events often happen at home, in graveyards or in places such as Masonic temples or buildings where occult practices are performed over which they have obtained some legal right. Sometimes they will appear in what seems to be a dream.

One woman who came to me experienced such a presence only at night in the hallway outside her bedroom—but only occasionally when she did not expect it and her husband was away. The irregularity of the appearances, the fact that her husband was always away and that she had a small baby, all led her to become quite upset. In this case and several other similar ones, we discovered that the demonic beings had a claim to the place where they appeared.

This "right" often is based on some event that happened there. For example, "pagan" rituals such as chanting or sacrificing, fortune telling or other Satan-empowered events, the death of a demonized person, violence, and bloodshed. All may result in demons continuing their residence.

Such demonic activity may have a present cause if someone in the house gives permission. This invitation may come from a demonized person or be the outcome of occult activities, pornography, satanically empowered music, or other activity empowered by the Enemy. Artifacts dedicated to enemy gods (spirits), have demons in them. Tourists and military personnel often bring from overseas, authentic (as opposed to merely tourist) images or implements used in pagan rituals or dedicated to gods or spirits.

Boldness may lead demons to speak audibly, or nearly audibly, inside the heads of people. Usually they can be fairly sure the persons will assume their problem is psychological and blame themselves, thus allowing the demons to go undetected. Demons can, however, misjudge the person they are tormenting and end up getting cast out.

When evil spirits are confident of their control, they may take over the person's body and cause shaking, fainting, blackouts, and fits. They can also cause people to speak in other voices. Such manifestations also sometimes occur when demons are confronted in the power of the Holy Spirit.

2. Evil spirits often make mistakes. The kinds of demonic boldness described above can be mistakes if the persons involved know how to recognize them and go on the attack. This happened with the pastor who came to me describing voices he had been hearing in his head for some time. The demons probably felt the pastor would respond to the voices in fear, self-accusation, resignation, or in some other way that would strengthen their grip. They probably also assumed the pastor was so unaware of their presence that he would not do anything to disturb them. They miscalculated, however, and now they are gone.

Demons like to disrupt in a way that people don't recognize. Not infrequently, though, they miscalculate and attack people who understand how they work. That's when they get kicked out. I have ministered to several people who have experienced moderate to extreme difficulty in worship. Recognizing the work of the Enemy, we have often been able to bring freedom from demons who made the mistake of getting too bold with the wrong people.

3. Pressured by the power of the Holy Spirit, demons often incriminate themselves. In the chapters that follow, we will deal in detail with how to get demons out of a person. Here, though, we'll simply note that in the encounter between their power and bluff and the power of the Holy Spirit, demons frequently "freak out," come out of hiding, and reveal things against their will.

For example, when a demonized person is worshiping God, not infrequently the power of God forces the demons to reveal their presence by causing such things as shaking, physical pain, blanking out, or strange impulses (for example, a strong desire to run or thoughts of sexual activity). Similar things also happen when demons are challenged in the name of Jesus to release their grip on a person.

RESISTING DEMONIC INFLUENCES

Whether a demon is inside or outside, certain things can be done to weaken its grip. These tactics don't necessarily get out demons living inside. We will deal with that process later. But certain things can be done to shut down or weaken demonic activity (whether from inside or outside), at least temporarily.

1. Spiritual growth weakens Satan's ability to work in or on a person. I have asked several demons why they didn't have a stronger grip on the person. What they say can be summed up in the words of one of them: "She (or he) is too close to God." Growing spiritually, though often it doesn't seem to get the demon(s) out, does weaken them to the point where they are easily evicted when challenged in the name of Jesus. And I suspect many demons are withdrawn by their spirit supervisors when they are thus weakened.

To grow spiritually, we need to spend time with God both alone and in fellowship. Constant listening to and conversing with God "at all times" (1 Thes 5:17)—as friend with friend, as child with Father, as wife with husband—weakens the Enemy's grasp. So does worship—singing, praising, expressing love and dedication to our Lord and Savior. So does fellowship with believers. So do Bible reading and memorization. So does being joyful (Phil 4:4), filling our minds with good thoughts, and practicing Christian behavior (Phil 4:8-9). The Enemy is defeated or at least weakened when we behave as our King expects us to behave.

2. Demonic activity weakens when people give Jesus their heavy loads. Jesus says "all... who are tired from carrying heavy loads," are to come to him and receive the rest he promises (Mt 11:28) as we cast all our cares on him (1 Pt 5:7). It is especially important to give him the loads caused by our negative reactions to the hurts of life. We are to give him our anger, bitterness, and hateful feelings (Eph 4:17-32) and forgive others as we have been forgiven (Mt 6:14-15).

If we take care of the inner "garbage," the Enemy's ability to influence us either from outside or inside is considerably lessened. I believe the absence of "inner garbage" was what Jesus was referring to when he said, "The ruler of this world is coming, and *he has nothing in Me*" (Jn 14:30, NKJV). Many people can get rid of such garbage by themselves through prayer. Others need the assistance of someone skilled in inner healing. This will be covered in chapter seven.

3. In the name of Jesus, demons can be commanded to quit. As already mentioned, when I suspect Enemy involvement, I have found it helpful to say something like, "If this is the Enemy, I command you to stop in Jesus' name." Since I don't always know whether demons are involved, I include "If." But I am startled again and again at how often the activity ceases after I assume authority and command whatever emissaries of the Enemy may be present to stop what they are doing.

I live with the assumption that Satan and his followers are anxious to harass me, that they are constantly looking for ways either to induce things to go wrong or to piggyback on things that are already going wrong. So if I am snared in an argument, or am caught in heavy traffic on my way to an important appointment, or feel I am being cheated, or am frustrated in a search for something lost, or am being thwarted in travel arrangements—all these signal me to command evil spirits to get out of my affairs. Sometimes I say the words out loud, sometimes in my spirit. Either way, the Enemy hears what I say and obeys.

Now, not every problem goes away when I do this, probably because demons are not involved in every problem. Many times when I'm caught in heavy traffic, the traffic doesn't clear in response to my command. Recently, I was nearly an hour late for a speaking engagement because, though I had allowed enough time, the traffic was unusually heavy. And I don't always find things I've lost right away when I take this approach, though I usually do find them reasonably soon and with a good bit less frustration.

But quite a number of things have changed. Several times changes have come about in airports and on planes. Once when it looked like my wife and I would have to stay overnight because our plane missed a connection, the company scheduled a larger plane to accommodate the extra passengers—but only after I commanded any enemies to cease and desist. Perhaps it was chance. But perhaps my taking authority made a difference.

Bluffers that they are, demons know we Christians have more power available to us than they do. But they still try to put things over on us. And their strategy works, unless we remember who we are and make use of the authority we have.

4. Since Satan attacks through deception, one of our best defenses is truth. When we hear a lie in our mind and accept it, we give our Enemy a victory. When, however, we refuse the lie and assert the truth, he loses the battle.

When we hear the untrue negative thoughts demons plant in our minds concerning ourselves, others, God, or circumstances, we need to assert the truth. It is amazing how things change when we reject those thoughts and speak the truth. In response to "I'm worthless," let me suggest: "Not true. I reject that thought. The truth is, I am a child of the most high God...." In response to "After what you've done, you can't be forgiven that easily. God requires more than that before he grants forgiveness," try quoting and really standing on 1 John 1:9—the truth about how God deals with our sin. Or recall and assert to the Enemy Jesus' treatment of the woman caught in adultery (Jn 8) or Peter after his denials (Jn 21). In response to lies or exaggerations concerning others, refuse them and, in keeping with Philippians 4:8, assert about those persons "things that are good and that deserve praise: things that are true, noble, right, pure, lovely, and honorable."

Assert the truth that God offers acceptance rather than rejection. Assert forgiveness for yourself or others when the lie is condemnation. Assert love and acceptance when demons tempt you to hate and reject. Bless when demons tempt you to criticize or claim superiority over someone else. Assert scriptural truth concerning questions of what God is like and what he is accomplishing. Continually resist the Enemy by confronting his lies with God's truths. Eventually he will tire of attacking you with deceptions (Jas 4:7).

SIX

Demonic Attachment and Strength

WALKING IN THE WALLED CITY

An ancient part of Kowloon (a section of Hong Kong) has been called "the Walled City." While on a ministry trip a few years ago, a group of us toured this "city of darkness," escorted by an outsider who knows it well, Jackie Pullinger (see Pullinger, *Chasing the Dragon* and *Crack in the Wall*).

This six-and-a-half acre square city within a city consists of a tangle of shops, small factories and residences constructed several stories high, many made of what looked like temporary materials. We followed narrow pathways and stairways between and inside these structures to get to where we were going and never saw sunlight. I could never tell whether we were indoors or outdoors! Above our heads boxes dripped water and suspicious-looking wires carried electricity, both stolen, we were told, from sources outside the Walled City. Constantly beneath our feet was damp concrete, wood, or dirt covered with trash and sewage.

Darkness, dampness, and dirt were everywhere. The smells were awful. It seemed like a fitting place for the thousands of heroin addicts, fugitives, prostitutes, and the pimps and their customers who lived and worked there. Quite possibly, the

Walled City is one of the darkest, filthiest places in the world.

As we walked through the small passageways, trying not to step into the sticky trash and raw sewage, I thought, "I've never seen so much garbage in one place." As the thought crossed my mind, I became aware of another kind of inhabitant of the Walled City. It was full of rats! They scurried back and forth across our path with little fear of us. This was their territory, not ours. Jackie commented that rats were at least as numerous as people in the Walled City. This was no surprise—where garbage abounds, one is certain to find rats!

RATS AND GARBAGE

My experience in the Walled City is a parable of what we face when dealing with demons. The dank, dark, garbage-filled setting of the Walled City provides a picture of the kind of place demons like to inhabit. In this "city of darkness" rats were rampant because garbage was abundant. Inside a human being, emotional or spiritual garbage provides just such a congenial setting for demonic rats.

Wherever emotional or spiritual garbage exists, demonic rats seek and often find entrance. If the dark city is torn down and the garbage disposed of, the rats cannot stay. The solution to the rat problem in the Walled City, then, is not to chase away the rats. It is to dispose of the garbage. So it is with demons. *The biggest problem is not the demons, it is the garbage.*

As should be obvious by now, demons are most frequently attached to damaged emotions or sin. If there is sin it is usually the result of an attitude stemming from emotional damage. Knowing this, I look for and deal with the emotional problems and gently lead the person to deal with any resulting sin, such as unforgiveness, without necessarily calling it sin. I approach things in this gentle way for at least two reasons: (1) I believe it is a more realistic approach than the frantic search for sin that has become standard, and (2) I believe it is both untrue and damaging to imply (as many do) that it is the sinfulness of the person that has caused the demonization. It seldom is.

Since demons are usually attached to emotions, they commonly have names related to their emotional base. These are what we call their "function" names. They may also have personal names. In dealing with demons through inner healing as I do (see chapter seven), it is most useful to know their function names, since it is those names that indicate the emotion or attitude in need of correction to weaken and evict the demon.

Demons operate most often in groups, seldom singly. They are organized hierarchically, however, with one leader in charge of each group. My practice is to discover the head "rat," and by the power of the Holy Spirit, to bind to him all demons under his control. This enables me to deal with the entire group at the same time, because the head spirit speaks for all of them. However, more than one group of spirits may be in a person, with a head spirit over each group with power equal to that of the other heads. It is usually possible, then, once each group has been bound to its head spirit, to bind all the groups together. More on this in chapter nine.

Demons cannot live in a person unless two conditions exist: (1) they must have discovered an "entry point," an emotional or spiritual weakness through which they can enter, and (2) they must have a "legal right," a right that accords with the laws of the spiritual universe, allowing them to be there. Both are provided when the host does not deal with the sins, attitudes, and behaviors mentioned in chapter three. Ignoring such problems litters the passageways of a person's being with trash to which demons are attracted. Failure to honestly face and handle sins and unhealthy attitudes weakens a person's system, giving demons an entry point. Wallowing in the sins and attitudes gives them a legal right to be there.

Jim was hurt badly as a child by many adults. His grandmother and a hired man regularly beat him. The latter abused him sexually as well. Jim's natural and understandable reaction was to be angry at them and others who had mistreated him. When Jim came to me for ministry at about age forty-five, inside him was a seething jumble of hateful emotions that sometimes erupted into incidents when he would lose control and beat his wife. Intense guilt and remorse followed, accompanied by extreme frustration over his lack of self-control. His violence had ruined three previous marriages, and his fourth appeared headed for divorce as well. He was angry at himself, his abusers, and God, and he could find no relief.

Though Jim's childhood reactions were normal and, to some extent, necessary for survival, retaining them had weakened his system and given a demon of rage both an entry point and a legal right to live in him. The festering of the wounds in his emotions and spirit provided plenty of garbage for Rage and a host of other demons to feed on. And as long as Jim did not deal with these attitudes and did not forgive those who had hurt him, Rage and the others had a strong grip on him.

Since I don't like to deal with demons when they are strong, I worked with Jim to heal the wounds and thus weaken the demons through inner healing. I asked the Holy Spirit to take Jim back to one event after another, to allow him to feel again the hurt he felt as a child and to experience the presence of Jesus who protected and helped him to survive in each event. Under the power and guidance of the Holy Spirit, then, I led him to see his abusers as victims themselves. He was enabled to understand the truth that he was not bad, guilty, or deserving of the abuse, and he was helped to forgive those who hurt him as Jesus had forgiven those who hurt him (Lk 23:34). In the process, Jim was also able to forgive himself for not being able to gain control of the turbulent emotions that had pushed him to assault his wives, as well as a brother. He also forgave God for letting these horrible things happen to him.

Only after this internal work did I challenge the demons.

By then, the spirits that had pushed him so often to violence had become quite weak. As Rage commented, "Ooooh, I'm in trouble now!" Jim had no one left that he hadn't forgiven, no more anger at his grandmother, the hired man, himself, God, or anyone else. So the demons had no more garbage to feed on and couldn't offer much resistance when commanded to leave. Both entry point and legal right had been taken from them. When the garbage was dealt with, the rats were easy to get out. And, unless Jim opens himself up again by reclaiming the harmful attitudes, those rats will be easy to keep away.

FUNCTION NAMES OF DEMONS

As I indicated earlier, demons have names that signify their functions. Thus, most demon names are the names of emotions. A selection of the names you might find in typical clusters follows (see Hammond & Hammond, *Pigs in the Parlor*, for a similar but more complete listing). Note that there is the repetition. Also, I have used italics for the names of demons that usually head the group.

- *Death*, suicide, murder
- *Destruction*, violence
- *Darkness*, deceit
- *Rage*, anger, hate
- *Hate*, revenge, murder
- *Unforgiveness*, anger, bitterness, resentment
- *Rebellion*, stubbornness
- *Rejection*, self-rejection, fear of rejection
- *Fear*, terror, torment, fear of... (for example, rejection, pain, dark, being alone, being outdoors, heights)
- *Self-rejection*, inadequacy, unworthiness, perfectionism
- *Guilt*, shame, embarrassment, sensitivity
- *Worry*, anxiety, worry about... (for example, future, the impression one makes)
- *Deceit*, lying

- *Confusion,* frustration, forgetfulness
- *Criticism,* condemnation, judgmentalism, faultfinding
- *Adultery,* seduction
- *Rape,* violence
- *Depression,* anger, defeat
- *Nervousness*
- *Sensitivity,* fear
- *Doubt,* unbelief, skepticism
- *Pride,* arrogance, vanity
- *Perfection,* insecurity
- *Competition,* insecurity, pride
- *Infirmity,* sickness (may be a specific disease such as *cancer, diabetes, arthritis* or the like)
- *Blasphemy,* cursing, mockery

In addition to such "emotion" demons, others encourage compulsions and addictions. These may go by such names as:

- *Compulsiveness* or *compulsion*
- *Control,* domination, possessiveness
- *Performance,* pleasing others
- *Intellectualism,* need to understand, rationalization
- *Religiosity,* ritualism, doctrinal obsession
- *Lust,* sexual impurity, adultery
- *Pornography,* sexual fantasy
- *Homosexuality,* lesbianism
- *Masturbation* (obsessive)
- *Alcohol*
- *Drugs*
- *Nicotine*
- *Gluttony*
- *Anorexia*
- *Bulimia*
- *Caffeine*

Occult and cult spirits (including those of false religions) are another category. These often can be quite powerful. Some to look for are:

- *Freemasonry*
- *Christian Science*
- *Scientology*
- *Jehovah's Witness*
- *New Age*
- *Rosicrucianism*
- *Unity*
- *Mormonism*
- *Ouija Board*
- *Horoscope*
- *Witchcraft*
- *Astrology*
- *Fortune Telling*
- *Palmistry*
- *Water Witching*
- *Buddhism* and various Buddhist spirits
- *Islam* and various Islamic spirits
- *Hinduism* and various Hindu spirits
- *Shintoism* and various Shinto spirits

STRENGTH OF ATTACHMENT

A variety of factors contribute to the strength of the grip a demon has on the person in which he lives:

1. Demons differ in strength. Some demons appear to be inherently stronger than others. Occult demons and those coming through inheritance, for example, seem to be inherently stronger than those attached to emotions. Some of my toughest battles have been with demons of Freemasonry. Likewise, those invited consciously or empowered through cursing seem to have a stronger grip than those picked up during life experiences. Furthermore, demons enforcing compulsions seem usually to be stronger than those attached to emotions.

2. The amount of "garbage" a demon has to "feed on" is an important variable. If a demon is attached to a lot of hurt, it will be quite strong. When there is less hurt for it to be attached to, it will be weaker. If it is very weak, apparently it may leave, even without being commanded to, if permitted by its superior to do so. However, I once asked a very weak demon why it didn't leave, given the fact that it had so little grip on the person. It replied, "I have not been allowed to."

3. Demons seem organized in hierarchical groupings with one as the leader. In my experience, it is rare to find only one or two demons in a person. In a typical ministry session we first make contact with one of the lesser demons in the group, say, lust. Lust may have three or four demons under him (for example, sexual perversion, fantasy, and deceit). But either by his admission or by word of knowledge, we find a spirit of anger over lust, and a spirit of fear over anger. Fear may be toward the top of the hierarchy, with two or three others (such as rejection, abandonment, and pornography) between him and lust. Above fear, we may find demons with names like rage, destruction, darkness, and death, any of which could be the leader of the group.

4. Among non-occult demons, certain ones are more likely to be head demons than others. For example, if there is a spirit of death, he is likely to be in charge. Destruction or darkness often will be in charge also and sometimes rejection or fear, especially if there is no spirit of death.

Any of these spirits can function under an occult demon. Frequently, however, I have found an occult demon to be approximately equal in power to a spirit such as death, and to have a separate group of demons under him. In ministering to Jim, I found an American Indian spirit to be in charge of one group while Rage was in charge of another.

5. Inside spirits are under the authority of higher level spirits outside. Demons often are sent inside a person by higher level spirits outside and, apparently, are not free to leave until the outside spirits allow or are forced to let them go. For this reason it is good to begin every ministry session by breaking any authority or ability to help, of the higher level spirits outside the person.

6. A person's actions can weaken the demons inside him. Demons inside a person are weakened by that person's spiritual growth. When demonized Christians make choices that draw them closer to Christ, the demons lose ground. Several demons, asked why they didn't have a stronger grip on the person they lived in, have told me, "She's too close to God. I can't get her."

Worship, prayer, Bible reading, and Christian fellowship seem to suppress demons, at least temporarily. Choosing to deal with sin or emotional hurts seems to result in permanent weakening of the demons attached to those problems.

A very important weakening technique is prayer by others. Demons often speak of the amount of protection God gives a person as limiting their ability to influence. Sometimes they speak of the number of angels assigned to protect the person. A combination of spiritual growth and prayer both protects the person and impairs the ability of demons to do their work. Those in deliverance ministries require much prayer as we plunder the Enemy's camp.

The most dramatic example I've heard of prayer affecting the work of demons was told by Elizabeth Mahoney. She was a New Age devotee who not only had a healing ministry, but taught others to channel and minister healing in the power of the spirits she served. Through the concern of some friends of her mother who were Christians, however, a prayer campaign was launched for "Tiz." As a result, she wrote:

> At first gradually, and then with increasing speed, everything I had worked so hard for began to deteriorate. The spirits became cold and distant. Channeling sessions became painful, leaving me sick and exhausted.... I was becoming so weak that I couldn't hold down a job....
>
> My friends were shocked to find that I couldn't just heal myself. I was the one who people usually came to for help, I had no one to turn to. When I asked the spirits for help,

they answered me only with silence.

During a meditation, one of my "guides" spoke to me for the last time. He informed me that none of "them" could stay with me any longer....

"You belong to a higher authority," they said angrily and agitatedly. "One much more powerful than we."

"Who is he? How will I find him?" I begged them.

"He is so powerful that we cannot even utter his name," they answered. Then weeks of silence followed. I was lost, confused, and frightened.[1]

Tiz now knows that the prayers of lots of people she didn't even know crippled the evil spirits and led to her escape from their grip.

7. A person's actions can strengthen the grip of demons. The more a person gives in to temptations or to emotions being reinforced by the demons, the stronger the demons get. Or, if during a deliverance session a person gives up fighting the demon because the pain or discomfort is so great, that demon gains strength and wins the battle. Likewise, if a person gets rid of a demon but later invites him back in, the demon comes in stronger than when he left, and perhaps with others (Lk 11:26).

WHAT DEMONIC STRENGTH MEANS

Some of what the word "strong" means when applied to demons will have become obvious by now. Nevertheless, it will be helpful to summarize what we mean when we talk of demonic strength.

One indication of a demon's strength is how much control of the person he can take. At the weaker end of the scale, many demons don't seem to be able to exert anything approaching control. They have to be content with harassing the person. Illustrations of three levels of harassment or control follow:

1. Harassment by a weak spirit. A woman who was invaded by a spirit of fear when raped may experience a surge of fear whenever she encounters a man who reminds her of her attacker, or whenever she recalls the rape or hears a report of one in the media. Through counseling (without deliverance) and through her own spiritual growth, she may have dealt with the issue enough to decrease the strength of the demon so that it barely bothers her at all.

2. A measure of control by a spirit with more strength. Another rape victim who contracted one or more demons (such as anger, fear, pain) during the rape, but has not been able to work through her emotions, may experience some times being out of control. For example, she may find that while disciplining her children, she gets "carried away" by her anger and seriously overdisciplines them. Or she may find herself disturbingly overcome with a mixture of emotions for no apparent reason when her husband makes love to her. Or she may find herself compulsive about her need to bathe, especially after sexual intercourse.

In such a case, the demons are able to exert a measure of control at certain times and in certain situations. The person may be puzzled by the lack of self-control, but not enough to suspect external interference. Any number of women have complained to me about losing control when correcting their children, but they have no problems with self-control otherwise. Often their problem is solved through inner healing—that is, dealing with events in their own childhood in which their emotions were damaged. Often, however, these hurts have given opportunity for a demon to enter and it is his ability to influence her behavior that pushes her out of control.

Notice the large difference between the amount of demonic influence in this example and that in the first. The second rape victim had not dealt with the resulting garbage. Each may have experienced the same degree of invasion initially, but the grip of the demons was weakened in the first instance through the woman's dealing honestly and effectively with her damaged emotions.

3. An even greater measure of control by an occult spirit. As already pointed out, occult spirits tend to have a stronger grip than those attached to emotions. I had the privilege of ministering to a delightful pastor's wife whom I'll call Lori. She was in her mid-thirties. Her father and mother had been involved in Freemasonry for most of their lives. Lori had belonged to Rainbow Girls, an affiliate of Freemasonry, as a teenager. When she became a Christian, however, her involvement waned, not because she knew the danger of it but because her Christian activities were more meaningful.

After we had worked with Lori for about twenty-five hours over the course of a week, she was finally free of the spirit of Freemasonry and the several dozen other spirits that the head spirit had invited in. She was so changed that her husband declared, "I have a brand new wife!" As Lori compares her new self to her old, she is able to pinpoint areas in which demons exerted a disturbing amount of control. For example, for the first time in her life she can think clearly.

She is now able to work toward loving herself, whereas previously even the thought of self-love was unimaginable. With the ability to love herself has come the capacity to appreciate, love, and make friends with her three children. She also can stop resenting her husband and his ministry, and instead, actively endorse and give herself to it. And for the first time in their marriage she can accept her husband's love and give herself fully to him. Lori is truly a new being.

Though before her deliverance, Lori was able to fool most people into thinking she was okay, those close to her saw her unhappiness and sense of unworthiness. These feelings seemed to stem from the control the spirit of Freemasonry and his friends were able to exert over her. Lori had not experienced the kind of childhood abuse that causes others great problems, but she did have feelings of abandonment by her parents. The garbage in Lori's life accumulated after the demon came, rather than providing the occasion for the demon's entrance, for her head demon had come by inheritance. Probably for that reason, he was able to continually exert quite a bit of control over her.

Each of these examples is typical of dozens I've encountered. Even the last example in which the head demon was inherited and invited dozens of others in is typical of a large number of persons God has led my way.

STRENGTH OF ATTACHMENT SCALE

I find it helpful to think of the strength of a demon's attachment to a person on a scale of 1-10.[2] Level one represents the weakest attachment and ten, the strongest. *I am using this scale here only to measure demonization in Christians.* To plot the strength of demonization in non-Christians (that is, persons in whose spirits demons can dwell), would require either a larger scale, say, of 1-15, or separate scales for Christians and non-Christians.

The demonization cases that attracted the attention of the writers of the Gospels strike me as all "heavy duty." Even those who were in a saving relationship with God (as I feel the "daughter of Abraham" was, in Lk 13:10-17), I would put in the 9-10 category. If some were not in a saving relationship with God, they might score higher on a scale of 1-15.

On several occasions it is recorded that many with illnesses and demons were brought to Jesus and he healed them all (see Lk 5:15; 6:18-19; 7:21). Among those in these groups who were freed from demons, there must have been many who had levels of demonization considerably lower than those whose stories are detailed.

People in Jesus' day were well-acquainted with demonization. Indeed, many among them (other than Jesus' disciples) were able to cast demons out by the power of God (Lk 11:19). What surprised them and attracted them to Jesus was not deliverance, but the authority and immediacy with which he freed people (Lk 4:36). It is understandable, then, that the Gospel writers recorded only a few spectacular cases.

My point is, I assume that most of the demons Jesus and his followers encountered in believers were, like most of those we encounter today, at the lower end of a scale of 1-10. We may picture such a scale like this (with thanks to John Wimber and Blaine Cook for suggesting the idea):

W e a k	M e d i u m	S t r o n g
1 2 3	4 5 6 7	8 9 10

As already made clear, our strategy in dealing with demons is to weaken any that are at medium or strong levels before seriously attempting to get them to leave. Thinking of that process leads us to see the above scale as a kind of meter or gauge with a needle pointing to the number representing the level of the demon's strength. Our strategy can then be pictured as attempting to move the needle down from, say, a 7 to a 1 or 2 during the inner healing part of any given deliverance session.

With this in mind, we find that demons who once were stronger but now have been weakened do not always fit the following characterizations of demons at each level. For example, demons who start out at a level 1 or 2 seldom have enough strength to use the person's vocal cords. Demons that have been weakened from, say, a 7 or 8 who have been speaking audibly through the person, however, tend to retain their ability to speak in that way even when weakened to level 1 or 2. It is, though, usually easy to observe the considerable lessening of vocal strength that occurs when a demon is thus weakened.

The following very rough characterizations of demons at each level apply to what we have observed when we first come upon them at that level, not necessarily to those who have been downgraded.

Levels 1–2: Demons at these levels are very weak and have very little control over a person, though they can be pesky in their harassment. They do such things as make a person feel uncomfortable in worship or Bible study, affect dreaming, apparently lower a person's resistance to illness, and perhaps contribute to misjudgment and confusion.

When challenged in the name of Jesus, they may cause the person to cough, feel sleepy, yawn, feel pain in some part of the body, or experience mild choking. They do not communicate audibly but through impressions and sometimes pictures in the person's mind. Demons at this level usually go fairly easily and in a short time.

Levels 3–4: At these levels demons can exert more control over their host. They can cause uncontrollable anger, fear, and greater discomfort in worship at times accompanied by near-panic and a strong desire to run. People with demons at this level frequently ask themselves, "Whatever made me do that?" They can experience an occasional, disturbing incident that causes them to question their competence and perhaps even their sanity. Thoughts of suicide are not uncommon, nor are recurring physical ailments.

When challenged in Jesus' name, demons at this level can act pretty cocky and arrogant. They can put up a bit of a fight if challenged before they are weakened, perhaps even shaking the person a bit, affecting breathing, causing confusion, causing physical pain. Clients have described them as "grabbing," as with claws, the throat, neck, or back of the head. Demons at this level, are able to communicate quite clearly either to the person's mind or, if the person will allow it, through using the person's voice. It is fairly easy for the person to keep such audible communication from happening, however, especially when "freaked out" by the experience. If you attempt to cast out demons at this level, you can expect a fairly long fight. It is preferable to weaken them to a lower level first.

Levels 5–6: Demons at these levels specialize in compulsive behavior. As the wife of a pastor delivered of a demon at this level said, "Everything my husband did was compulsive." These demons have greater control over their hosts and for longer periods of time. If there are spirits of anger or fear or hate, the person's personality will be slanted in those directions. Allergies and other nagging physical problems may also be present. If sexual perversions such as pornography and compulsive masturbation are present, they will be strong and guilt-producing. Demons at this level may become daring and speak in the person's mind in a way that would obviously indicate their presence if the person knew enough to look for them. They often try to convince their hosts that they are crazy. Strong thoughts of suicide and, for some, weak attempts to end it all are also characteristic.

When challenged at full strength, demons at this level can put up quite a fight. Unless forbidden to, they will cause bodily distortions and much pain in their attempts to get the deliverance stopped. They can throw people around and perform moderate feats of strength. They can also interfere with inner healing aimed at weakening their grip. They can make use of the person's vocal apparatus fairly easily unless the person works hard to suppress their vocalizations. If they interfere in the inner healing, it may be good strategy to challenge them, forbid them to cause violence and force them to reveal what they are attached to. Once this is known, then, the person can be led to deal with it thus weakening the demons.

Levels 7–8: *Rarely do we find Christians demonized at this high a level unless they have been involved in the occult.* Demons at these levels are able to exert a lot of control over their victims, sometimes for long periods of time. At this level of demonization, persons may seem to have two or more quite different personalities. When the demons take control, it is common to observe a disturbing glaze to the eyes, as well as violent or other uncharacteristic behavior that the person may be ashamed of later. More likely, the person probably will not remember the event very clearly, if at all. If the person is a Christian, the frequency of demonic control will likely be lessened and the ability to assert control enhanced.

At this level, if the demons are challenged at full strength, a lot of violence can result, even when the demons have been forbidden to cause it. No challenge at this or any other level should, however, be attempted without forbidding violence. "Acting out" also may take place at this level (for example, homosexual gestures, snakelike writhing). At this level, too, demons may strongly interfere as we attempt to weaken them through inner healing. Indeed, it may be very difficult to get clear access to the person's will, given the amount of demonic interference. The demons will, of course, be able to speak quite easily through the person's vocal cords, often without the person being able to curb them much. Sometimes the demons will speak in another voice.

Levels 9–10: *Rarely, if ever, are Christians demonized at this level.* At this level, the characteristics of level 7-8 are all to be found and often escalated. That is, demonic control will be greater and occur more often.

Challenging demons at this level at full strength is definitely not advisable. It may, however, be unavoidable, since they may be strong enough to keep the person off-balance a good bit of the time. Fasting, praying, and helping the person work on spiritual growth, strength of will, and root issues should be major parts of the strategy. Challenging the demons enough to get information from them should be tried as well.

AWARENESS

Westerners who are demonized rarely suspect this kind of interference can exist in their lives. This lack of awareness is aided by a worldview that discounts the reality of evil spirits (see Kraft, *Christianity with Power*). And Western churches, thoroughly infected by the same worldview assumptions, seldom give more than lip-service to the existence of Satan and demons. Thus demonic interference is almost always interpreted naturalistically as an emotional problem. And the person takes full blame for the problem.

This unawareness, accompanied by the practice of blaming ourselves for demonic as well as non-demonic problems, plays right into the hands of the Enemy. He is ecstatic when he can do his work without being blamed for it or even suspected of being present. This is one reason he is delighted when people believe that demons cannot inhabit Christians. In groups where that belief is held, he can go unnoticed, regularly and effectively influencing those who can hurt him most, Christians.

Those demonized at the lower levels may be especially unaware of the presence of intruders. They may feel pushed in negative ways from time to time and interfered with in worship, prayer, and Bible study. But, given prevalent teaching in Christian circles, they will blame their sin nature and not look further for a cause. Though the demons are weak and the harassment at a comparatively low level, I find the amount of self-condemnation generated by people with weak demonization can be very disturbing. They often become convinced that something is permanently wrong with them spiritually. Not infrequently, they question whether or not they are born again.

It is true that we are to take responsibility for whatever our spiritual, emotional, and physical condition is. The Scriptures give us no right to escape our responsibility by blaming Satan or demons. But the Scriptures were written to people who knew the Enemy's devices (2 Cor 2:11). They were not intended to offer all of the kinds of help needed by most American Christians today. For, unlike the people to whom those documents were addressed, most of us are almost totally unaware of how the Enemy works. *Though we need to take full responsibility for what happens within us, an important prior responsibility is to know how the Enemy works and what to do about it.*

At the middle levels of demonization, Western Christians usually miss detecting the indications of demons. Even though compulsiveness and lack of control can at times be troublesome, the likely response would be to blame the sin nature or emotional damage entirely. At this level, the person is likely to seek the help of a psychologist. But even Christian psychologists usually do not deal with demons. They usually work naturalistically without either the knowledge or the power it takes to free people from demons.

If the person faces the problems the demons are attached to, even though the psychologist is unaware of their presence, the demons' power gets weakened and at least some of them may leave on their own, if permitted by their leader. Rarely, however, do they all leave. The stronger ones need to be challenged and banished quite pointedly.

At the higher levels of demonization, the person may be out of control so much of the time that it is quite obvious to all that something is drastically wrong. Many of these people end up on the streets or in mental or criminal institutions. Some, however, are able to control themselves in public most of the time. Even at this level, though, our country's naturalistic worldview keeps most Americans from understanding the demonic part of their problems.

One point that needs to be mentioned is that some people seem to have a greater ability than others to resist demonic influence. Even some with a comparatively high level of infestation seem to be able to hide their symptoms well. Others, however, with a comparatively low level of interference seem to fall apart. I don't know why this is. It seems to be related to the strength of a person's will to fight. But what enables some to be strong in their willingness to fight while others are weak-willed, I don't understand.

While we need to be careful not to go to the extreme of blaming everything on demonization, we also need solid instruction concerning the important role demons play in sabotaging lives. It is heartening to see more attention being given to this subject by balanced Christian leaders. Addressing the reality of demons should not continue to be associated only with the "lunatic fringe."

SEVEN

Dealing with the Garbage through Inner Healing

GARBAGE FIRST, THEN DEMONS

When I hear people referring to a "deliverance ministry," I like to stop them to see what they understand by that term. What I find is that what we do in delivering people from demons is different from most.

Many in deliverance go after the demons right away. That approach presents at least two problems. First, it challenges the demons when they are strong. This can result in a big fight that is not good either for the deliverance team or for the person in whom the demons live. Second, the amount of what I'm calling garbage may be so great that the person is a sitting duck either for the banished demons to come back or for others like them to take advantage of the situation.

When the demons are dealt with first, people often assume that all or most of the work is done. Being freed from demons feels and looks so good that it is easy to neglect the need for inner healing. The demons may be gone but the most important part of the healing hasn't taken place and the person is at risk of being reinfested, perhaps by more demons than before (Lk 11:26).

So we refuse to see our task as simply deliverance. We have

found that the most important aspect of a deliverance ministry is never the casting out of the demons. The aim is healing. But the healing isn't complete until the deep level hurts that disrupt a person's relationship with God, self, and others are worked through under the power of the Holy Spirit. Such healing is commonly called inner healing. Other names are healing of memories, empowered ministry, or prayer counseling.

A woman I'll call Jane was brought to me by her concerned brother. She's in her mid-thirties, and her life had "dysfunctional" written all over it. She described a marriage she hated, a relationship with her children that was meaningful but marred by her angry outbursts, a childhood and earlier marriage marked by hurt, abuse, jealousy, resentment, and fear. Jane and some of her children also had disturbing physical problems. She had consulted with several psychologists and had given up on them.

From what Jane and her sister shared with me, it seemed *very* likely that she was demonized. She feared that she might be, though she had believed the myth that Christians couldn't be demonized. However, like many who believe that myth and also suspect they might have demons, she has found it difficult to be sure she is saved.

The question I faced with Jane, as with all others, was "Where should I start?" After my usual prayer in which I asked the Lord to show me where to start, we began. Over three hours later, we ended the session without having challenged the demons. We probed and prayed through quite a number of the wounding events in her past. We worked on anger, resentment, jealousy, and fear, and also led Jane to forgive everyone she remembered who had hurt her.

As I have indicated several times, that is the way to weaken any demons that might be present. It also is the way to bring healing to the badly wounded parts, whether or not demons are involved. This is typical of my approach to anyone who comes.

On Jane's second visit, with her permission, I challenged some demons and by the power of the Holy Spirit was able to release her from them. The change was so great that she reported she was going through an identity crisis as she was learning how to live in the newness that became possible when she dealt honestly with her inner pain in the power of Jesus. The demons were an important factor. Indeed, they were running her a merry chase as long as Jane had a lot of unresolved emotions on which they could feed. With many of those healed, however, they were kicked out comparatively easily.

Jane still has quite a bit of work to do. But with her, as all others, the most important part of the work is the inner healing, not getting rid of the demons.

WHAT INNER HEALING IS

Inner healing or, as I prefer to call it, *deep-level healing,* is a ministry in the power of the Holy Spirit aimed at bringing healing to the whole person. Since the majority of human ailments are closely tied to damage in the emotional and spiritual areas, inner healing focuses there. It seeks to bring the power of Christ to bear on healing the roots from which damage springs. Since these are often in the memories carried unconsciously by those who come for help, inner healing involves a special focus on what is sometimes called "the healing of the memories." Specific problems often encountered are unforgiveness, anger, bitterness, rejection, low self-esteem, fear, worry, and sexual issues.

Two additional definitions of inner healing are those of Tapscott and Seamands:

Inner healing is the healing of the inner [person]: the mind, the emotions, the painful memories, the dreams. It is the process whereby we are set free from feelings of resentment, rejection, self-pity, depression, guilt, fear, sorrow, hatred, inferiority, condemnation, or worthlessness, etc. Romans 12:2 (KJV) says, "And be not conformed to this world: but be ye transformed by the renewing of your mind..." Inner healing is the renewing of your mind.[1]

Inner Healing is a form of Christian counseling and prayer which focuses the healing power of the Spirit on certain types of emotional/spiritual problems.[2]

As we go through life, we get hurt. Indeed, most of us have been hurt so much that if we had a small bandage on our bodies for every time we've been hurt, we'd look like mummies! When we are hurt, we do our best to keep from falling apart or reacting in such a way that our behavior is socially unacceptable. Either way, we suppress our honest (truthful) reaction.

Suppressing these reactions, while it enables us to cope at the time, becomes counterproductive later. When we suppress our true reactions, it is like putting bandages on open, unhealed wounds without cleansing them first. Those wounds, then, though bandaged, become infected and fester under the bandages. But the bandages leak, allowing the infection to affect our lives long after the cause may have disappeared from our conscious memory.

Ideally, we would have dealt honestly with each hurt at or soon after the time it happened. This is done by facing our true feelings, admitting them, and allowing Jesus to take charge. He has invited us to come to him with all of our heavy loads (Mt 11:28). We are further admonished by Paul to deal with our anger and, presumably, other such reactions before the end of every day (Eph 4:26). Above all, as both Jesus and Paul made plain, we are to forgive anyone who has hurt us (Mt 6:14-15; Eph 4:32).

The fact that we have ordinarily not kept such "short accounts" with our hurts, leaving them to fester within us results in mild to severe disruption in three relationships: with God, with ourselves, and with others. Disruptions in these areas create most of the garbage the Enemy takes advantage of. Bringing healing in those areas breaks the Enemy's grip on us.

The ideal *relationship with God* would see us as new and growing creatures (2 Cor 5:17), united with the Lord and one with him in spirit (1 Cor 6:17), filled with the Holy Spirit (Acts 2:4) and living as close to the Father as Jesus did (Jn 5:19, 30).

The ideal *relationship with self* would see us accepting, loving, and forgiving ourselves as God accepts, loves, and forgives us. We would then see ourselves as full-fledged children of God (1 Jn 3:1; Rom 8:14-17; Gal 4:4-7), heirs with Jesus of all that God has for him, and holding our heads high as his princes and princesses. Such a relationship frees us to totally forgive any who hurt us.

The ideal *relationship with others*, would see us as accepting, loving, and forgiving others as God accepts, loves, and forgives them, and as he has enabled us to accept, love, and forgive ourselves. We relate in a healthy, constructive manner with all others, and especially Christians—free of envy, judging, and other negative emotions. We also relate properly to all God-ordained authority.

These are the ideals. The actual, however, is often far from these standards. So we find *spiritual illness* in our lives as the result of factors such as sin, neglect of our relationship with God, wrong views of God, and anger at God for what he allows to happen. In addition, we may have inherited a generational spirit or curse and be under satanic attack due to the garbage within us. These, too, can cause spiritual illness.

There may be *illness in our relationship with self* due to feelings of unworthiness or self-rejection usually stemming from childhood conditioning. This may be paralleled by self-condemnation, involving anger at oneself and a refusal to accept and forgive oneself. There may even be self-hate. In addition, intergenerational spirits and curses or satanic attacks can damage our relationship with ourself.

There may also be *sickness in our relationships with others.* Our individualism often keeps us from the right kind of closeness with others. Broken relationships, of course, bring relational illness. So do personal problems such as sin, an unhealthy self-image, and attitudes such as arrogance and a critical spirit. Intergenerational spirits and curses or satanic attacks also often play a role in disrupting relationships with others.

Such relational illnesses tend to show up in *emotional problems.* Our reactions to what others have done to us or what we have done to ourselves often result in damaging attitudes such as guilt, anger, bitterness, unforgiveness, and fear. Improper family conditioning often ushers in responses such as perfectionism, performance orientation, and a critical spirit.

Note that *it is the reaction, not the hurt itself that becomes the problem.* Wallowing in even a legitimate reaction, then, results in the build-up of the emotional garbage demons feed on. We often have the right to be angry or even take revenge. But Jesus knows if we hold onto that right, the inner infection will destroy us. So he says, "Give it to me." Having the feelings is not wrong, but keeping them will ruin us.

Such emotional illness is often signaled by a *fear of facing the past.* Our brains record everything that happens in our lives. However, they also hide and suppress the recall of the heavy stuff. This is helpful for immediate survival, but if it is kept buried, it infects the present. Many of us, however, have suppressed hurt for so long and know so little of what to expect if we let it surface that we respond with fear at the very suggestion of dealing with the past. And the Enemy is very active in encouraging such fear.

Yet we may find we overreact to small irritations. We experience depression that seems unrelated to present circumstances. We have weird dreams and experience strange sleep patterns. We often don't know what these things mean or what to do about them. Some go to psychologists. And a percentage of those gain control over such symptoms by dealing with the past. Yet for many it's frightening to think of exposing what's inside. Maybe, we reason, it won't work anyway. So fear and the thought of possible embarrassment keep many from seeking healing.

Hiding our inner stuff without dealing with it, however, affects the three relationships mentioned above. *With God* we are uncomfortable, especially if he gets close, for we expect him to punish and condemn us. We may be tormented by guilt, unworthiness, and fear of his judgment. *With self,* we find ourselves mired in feelings of inadequacy and self-rejection, unable to accept love, forgiveness, or acceptance from God or others. Nor can we love, forgive, or accept ourselves. Instead, we blame ourselves for whatever bad things happened to us, assuming they wouldn't have happened if we didn't deserve it. And often physical problems go along with these emotional difficulties. *With others,* we live in constant fear of discovery, assuming that if others or even God knew our past, they would not accept us. We keep people at a distance and live in loneliness, envy, and anger over the seeming differences between our situation and that of others.

God's way, however, is honesty and truth. He wants us to face the past squarely and deal with it with his help. He says, as northern Nigerians put it, "When it's time to bathe, don't try to hide your belly button!" When it's time to work toward healing, we must face and deal with everything. But we can deal with it with him and receive healing and freedom. Spiritual surgery, like physical surgery, is, however, often painful.

With Jesus, we can go back to the experiences in which we were hurt, both those we can recall and those our brain has recorded but doesn't allow us to recall. We can re-experience them with Jesus there, enabling us to forgive those who hurt us and to give our pain to him. The result is freedom from the bondage to the past that has crippled us and, if demons are there, provided them with the garbage they have been feeding on.

APPLYING THE PRINCIPLES

To illustrate the application of these principles, I present the following ministry which, though not a single event, is typical of numerous actual ministry experiences. We will picture the client as a young woman named Sue. We began with prayer, asking the Holy Spirit to take charge and lead all that was to happen. We also claimed his protection for all of us and our families from demonic attacks. Our prayer apparently roused a demon called Anger. As I tried to question Sue concerning her problems, Anger insisted on butting into our conversation. He seemed to be at about level 5 or 6 on our scale, so he had the strength to interfere. If the demon hadn't interrupted us, I would have paid no attention to him until the inner work had been done, even though, on the basis of what Sue told me of her reasons for coming, I strongly suspected his presence.

Anger started growling, threatened all sorts of nonsense, and tried to scare Sue by causing a pain in her back. So I took authority in the name of Jesus and commanded the demon to stop both the posturing and the pain. This made the demon angry, but he could do nothing about it. He had to stop most of what he was doing since our power was greater than his. Sue still experienced a bit of pain, but the demon's arrogant words and threats stopped completely.

Once the demon was thus bound, I began questioning Sue about her past. After a few minutes, she confessed she was harboring deep anger toward her husband in response to his constant verbal abuse throughout their marriage. After again asking the Holy Spirit to guide us, I led Sue to picture herself in one of those abusive situations. I asked Sue to let herself feel again her hurt and degradation, plus the anger she felt toward her husband at the time. I then invited Jesus to make himself visible to Sue by showing her where he was while she was being hurt.

As Sue put herself visually and emotionally into the situation, she was able to see Jesus standing near her with a sympathetic look on his face. His posture was such that Sue felt he would step between her and her husband to protect her at any time her husband attempted to strike her. As she pictured and felt the event, I began asking her to consider her husband's background. "Was he mistreated by the 'significant others' in his life?" I asked. "Could it be that he himself was a victim and has never gotten control of his own pain? People who have been victimized make victims of others," I said.

Sue admitted that her husband had indeed been victimized by his parents. It seemed he could do nothing right. They continually put him down when he was with them and criticized him behind his back. This criticism extended to his friends and now to his marriage. They made no secret of their disapproval of Sue. As we talked about her husband's background, Sue came to empathize with him. She was nearly overwhelmed with pity when she came to see her husband as a victim who could have been expected to function even more poorly, given the abuse he had experienced. With this realization, Sue easily found it possible to forgive him for passing on his own victimization to her.

As Sue pictured herself and the reality of Jesus' presence in the abusive situation, she forgave her husband *in the situation*. She followed that by dealing in the same way with several other situations and finally, at my suggestion, held out her hands to Jesus, allowing him to pile up in her hands all the unforgiveness, anger, and bitterness that had built up over the years. As she gave the pile of "garbage" to Jesus, she felt a considerable sense of freedom.

Sue was angry with other people as well. Among them was her father, who she felt had neglected and not affirmed her. She worked through forgiving him and the others also, sometimes going situation by situation, sometimes in a more general way. In each case, she was able to picture Jesus affirming her, releasing her from the guilt she felt over her anger and taking her burdens on himself. There were tears, first of anger, then of compassion, then of release. Sue felt as if an enormous burden had been lifted off her shoulders.

We spent about two hours dealing with Sue's anger, unforgiveness, and her tangle of damaged emotions: fear, self-rejection, depression, and discouragement. Then we called up the spirit of Anger again. He was now much weaker. We found he was the head of the group, with several demons under him. They had names like Rejection, Fear, Discouragement, and Envy. I commanded them all to be bound together with their head (Anger) and they were. This enabled me to kick them all out at once.

I commanded Anger, under the power of the Holy Spirit, to tell me if Sue still needed to forgive anyone. He said she still had something against her younger brother. I asked Sue to deal with that, and she did. I asked the demon if he still had anything on her. He said she hated herself. I helped Sue to see who she really is, a child of the King (1 Jn 3:1) and, therefore, a princess. This thought excited her and she was able to agree with Jesus that she was acceptable and forgivable and, on that basis, to choose to accept, forgive, and love herself. Once this was done, the spirit of Anger admitted that he and his cohorts had no more right to stay within her. And soon we got them to leave.

This is a typical example of how inner healing is essential in bringing total healing to the demonized person. Had I simply commanded the evil spirit to go the moment it appeared, we probably would have had a fight on our hands. And we might not have been able to get it out at all as long as all Sue's garbage was there. Had we gotten the demons out and left the garbage inside, Sue would have been in danger of reinfestation, or at least of having to continue life with wounds untouched by the healing power of God.

The deep hurt and anger at her husband, combined with unforgiveness and other emotional damage would have remained inside Sue, festering and hurting about as much as before. And she may well have concluded that her deliverance didn't work. Satan likes it when a delivered person isn't healed. Without the inner healing that provides the foundation for true freedom, deliverance only accomplishes a small part of what needs to be done.

INNER HEALING MINISTERS THE LOVE OF JESUS

Perhaps the most important reason to use inner healing during deliverance is that the process enables us to really demonstrate the love of Jesus. I can't overemphasize the fact that the main goal of deliverance, or any healing ministry, isn't simply to experience the power of Jesus or even to fight against and defeat the Enemy. It is to minister the love of Jesus. For *if what we do isn't loving, it isn't being done in Jesus' way.* And it is not, therefore, as healing as he intended it to be. Jesus used his power to show his love. So should we.

That is one reason I'm against "big shows" when doing deliverance. Allowing demons to inspire fear with violence, screaming, and vomiting is not a loving thing to do to the demonized person. When this happens, is it any wonder that many regret ever having let themselves in for the experience? And many shy away from deliverance, even when they're pretty sure they need it. Though in the biblical examples we sometimes see brief violence, it nowhere approximates the amount we see in some contemporary deliverance ministries. Instead, we see Jesus and his followers casting out demons calmly, showing love to the victims.

We practice inner healing not only because it is effective, but because it provides a loving way to minister to the wounded. I am constantly in awe of what Jesus does when we simply invite him to come and minister to those who hurt. Time and time again, he shows up in powerful, yet tender ways—touching the deep wounds within people in ways we could never imagine. He alone knows the deep pain buried within the hearts of those to whom we minister. When we call upon the Holy Spirit to guide, he usually gently leads from the less painful events to the more painful ones, healing each as he goes along.

As this takes place, trust in Jesus and intimacy with him is established or restored. This trust and intimacy become the base both for overall healing and for fighting the demons and their lies.

HELPFUL TIPS FOR ACCOMPLISHING INNER HEALING

I want to emphasize that there is no magic formula for relating inner healing to deliverance. It would be easy if we could hand out "six easy steps to inner healing." But we can't. The best we can do is to suggest some of the approaches we have found most helpful. These all have to be used according to the leading of the Holy Spirit and after he has been consciously invited to guide the ministry.

1. Invite Jesus to appear to the person within the situation. Before using this approach, we make it clear to clients that (1) we cannot explain why God allowed their abuse, but (2) we know Satan wanted to destroy them, yet (3) they were not destroyed. (4) This must mean that Someone more powerful than Satan was present, protecting them.

We then invite the person to forgive all who have hurt them and to picture Jesus in the situation in which the abuse happened. We point out that Jesus was indeed present and protecting them (otherwise the Evil One would have been able to destroy them), but that they were not able to see him when the event happened. They are usually able to see or feel Jesus' presence in the reliving and feel heartened as they are released from the pain of the loneliness they have lived with for many years.

2. A longer procedure we often use is to take the person back to the womb. This approach provides a means of dealing with certain problems in a general way and of uncovering others that need to be dealt with more specifically. It is based on the psychological theory that children in the womb are greatly affected by what their mother is feeling and thinking. We also assume that Enemy forces are actively attempting to destroy or damage babies before birth.

I often start this procedure with a technique I learned from one of my associates, Molly Sutherland-Dodd. I ask the person to picture Jesus' hands, with a sperm in one hand and an egg in the other. I then lead the person to voluntarily put Jesus' hands together, fertilizing the egg with the sperm to produce an embryo with the person's name on it. I suggest that God has been actively involved in every conception. Then I ask, "Do you think God made a mistake in allowing you to be conceived? Or in assigning you your gender?" Many people know or suspect that their parents did not want them or that they wanted them to be a different sex. If the person can choose with God not only to be, but to be the sex God has assigned, great healing can come to the person's self-image.

As people contemplate their conception, I will often feel led to take authority over the father's bloodline and then the mother's to break the power of and cancel all curses, dedications, spells, emotional problems, diseases, and any other satanic influence that may have been introduced into the person's inheritance. Often people will not feel any response. Sometimes, however, there is a feeling of release, probably indicating that something was broken. Even if there is no felt response, not infrequently we find out later that some power was indeed broken. Sometimes, though, we find later that some satanic power in one or both bloodlines does not get broken. I don't know why such power gets broken for some but not for others.

Next, we bless the child in each month of gestation, inviting the adult to see if any feelings come as we go along. Often the person gets a feeling of discomfort, loneliness, darkness, or something strong that lightens up as we go from month to month. One woman said she felt darkness, loneliness, and a sense of dread at the thought of coming into the world that turned to light and a strong desire to be born. As we go from month to month, the Holy Spirit often leads me to speak against negative attitudes that may have been passed along by the person's mother. Typical are anger, feelings of unworthiness, negative attitudes toward father or mother, fear, and harmful reactions from trauma while the person was in the womb. Many such attitudes are passed on from mother to child. If the person was a twin (that is, had a "wombmate"), negative attitudes toward the twin usually have to be dealt with.

Again, we ask clients to forgive anyone who is perceived as having hurt them and to give all negative emotions to Jesus. We bless the child in each month of gestation with such things as joy, peace, excitement about coming into the world, and the opposite of any negative emotions that come to their attention. If people feel they shouldn't have been born, it is good to lead them to say something like, "I choose life," several times during this process.

After blessing their ninth month, we invite people to picture their birth. Once born, we have them allow Jesus to pick them up and hold them as a baby. Often they can feel the pleasantness and security of Jesus' arms. I ask if the umbilical cord is still connected. If still connected, this usually signals some unhealthy attachment to mother or father that can be broken by inviting the person to enter the picture as an adult to cut and tie the cord. I then ask them to receive the baby from Jesus and to help the child to feel safe and secure in their arms just as they did when Jesus held them.

Not infrequently, people experience some difficulty re-experiencing their birth. This indicates something more needs to be done. Many find it difficult either to allow Jesus to hold them or to hold the baby themselves. A man once said to me, "I'm afraid I'll drop the baby." Most such problems relate (as did his) to feelings of unworthiness or of not feeling they have a right to be alive. It is good to stop when such things are said and deal immediately with any unforgiveness, anger, unworthiness, self-curses, and desire to die.

One man saw knives surrounding the picture of his birth. It turned out that he had a demon of hate. Another man saw the baby disintegrate and fall through his arms. This related to guilt and anger over an abortion his wife had had without his permission. Sometimes it does not become immediately clear why the interference has happened. If it is not clear, those who minister should store it in their memory and look for clues later in the ministry session. In the case of the man who saw the knives, it wasn't until considerably later in our session that we discovered what they meant.

After the person has re-experienced birth, I frequently ask the Holy Spirit to bring to the person's mind any other experiences that need to be dealt with. Frequently, childhood sicknesses and accidents must be worked through, often accompanied by times when the child was left in a hospital or with a caretaker and felt abandoned. Often it is helpful for persons to picture themselves as adults explaining things to themselves as children with Jesus looking on. One woman who had been regularly left with her grandparents for several days at a time, spent quite a bit of time accompanying her "inner child" through memory after memory in this way. The results were spectacular, both with respect to her inner healing and the weakening of the demons that were involved.

3. A useful procedure to use with miscarriages and abortions. This approach also can be modified and used effectively to help a person deal with the death of anyone close. I use it both for miscarriages and abortions experienced by the person or her husband and for any siblings that may have been lost in this way. Once life has been given, it is for eternity. And when the ones who have given it in some way lose it, the pain can be very great. So I have the person picture the baby, decide on its sex, give the child a name and talk to him or her as if the baby had been born. Sometimes apologies are in order, usually there is regret to talk about. But since parent and child will get to spend eternity together, it is fun to think of starting a relationship in this way.

I instruct people to hold and talk to the baby as long as they care to and then to give the baby lovingly to Jesus. In this way, parents agree to accept what Jesus has allowed to happen. They usually will see Jesus lovingly take the baby and disappear with him or her. One person saw Jesus carrying the diaper bag, bottles, and other paraphernalia as he walked away! This process is usually very freeing for those who have lost children or siblings. During this procedure a man whose older sister had been lost to miscarriage before he was conceived, realized that he had been living all his life with a guilty conscience over the loss of that child. Jesus freed him.

4. How to deal with adulterous relationships and other bonding of human spirits. I believe sexual relationships bond people spirit to spirit. If sexual relationships exist with persons other than one's marriage partner, that bonding will inhibit freedom. I first make sure all sin has been confessed and forgiven. Then I ask the person to picture the person(s) bonded with sexually and join me in saying something like, "I break my bonding with so-and-so and renounce any and all ties with that person that are empowered by satanic power." As we said this, one person who had been raped hundreds of times as a part of satanic rituals saw all of the men lined up like dominoes and fall down.

There are other bonding relationships that need to be broken in this way as well. Homosexual relationships, dominating relationships, and certain close friendships result in what some call "soul ties." If there is any suspicion that any of these are empowered by Satan, they need to be broken, using the same method as that for sexual ties.

The information in this chapter can be supplemented by reading any number of good books on inner healing. My own book on this subject is scheduled for publication in 1993. Meanwhile, for more popular approaches, let me suggest David Seamands, *Healing for Damaged Emotions, Healing of the Memories, Putting away Childish Things* and *Healing Grace,* as well as Betty Tapscott, *Inner Healing through Healing of Memories.* For a good treatment from a Roman Catholic perspective, try Dennis and Matthew Linn, *Healing Life's Hurts.* The most comprehensive presentations are, however, by John and Paula Sandford, *The Transformation of the Inner Man* and *Healing the Wounded Spirit.*

INNER HEALING TOGETHER WITH PROFESSIONAL COUNSELING

It will be fitting to end this chapter by underlining what I firmly believe concerning the relationship between inner healing and professional counseling. Though I believe the ideal would be for those with the full training of professional counsellors to work as we do in the power of the Holy Spirit, that ideal is seldom reached. Rather, many of us who have learned to do inner healing in the power of the Spirit, have not had the advantage of learning what counsellors know. Nor have most Christian counsellors had the opportunity to learn how to work as fully with the Holy Spirit as we could wish.

The twists and turns of helping people to get well are such that neither the trained nor those working in our way should feel they have no need of the other. Each set gets to rescue people who don't feel they were helped by the other set. Speaking for those of us without professional training, let me counsel humility. Though we may be marvelously gifted, we don't have all the answers. As one of the pioneers in inner healing has pointed out, "Inner healing is *one and only one* of such (healing) ministries; and should never be made the *one and only form,* for such overemphasis leads to exaggeration and misuse."[3]

Seamands makes a good point. Good Christian counseling, though it usually takes longer than inner healing, can be crucial in a person's movement toward wholeness. Even while this longer process is going on, however, inner healing (plus or minus deliverance) can function to produce "spurts" toward health at various points along the way. Christian counseling can be extremely effective in identifying painful issues and dealing with them to some extent. Nothing, however, is as healing as the power of the Holy Spirit applied to those issues. Yet there is great value in being expertly guided in the slower process of talking issues through and working in very human ways (guided by the Holy Spirit) to change basic behavioral patterns.

We advocate a combination of inner healing, deliverance, and solid Christian counseling for most people, but especially for those who have experienced extreme trauma, such as satanic ritual abuse in their early childhood. We need to be open to God working through many vehicles of healing. Both inner healing and counseling offer positive steps towards resolving deep level emotional pain. We recommend them both.

EIGHT

Getting Information from Demons

JULIE

We had reached an impasse! It was clear that Julie, a thirty-five-year-old missionary who had been suffering from depression for nearly a year, was inhabited by a demon. What was not clear was how to get it out. For one thing, the demon spoke only German, so we could not understand it. In fact, even Julie didn't understand some of the things the demon was saying through her own mouth! I had the feeling other demons might be there, but our attempts to get them to reveal themselves were not succeeding. And the Holy Spirit didn't seem to be showing us how to get through to them.

We had tried to do inner healing with Julie but were able to deal with only seemingly superficial things. We had spent several hours with her but had made only limited progress. I had the distinct impression that the demons had such a grip that they were preventing us from getting to the real issues. I decided, therefore, to go all out to get from the demons the information we needed.

So we increased the pressure on the demons in Julie to reveal more information to us. We were able by the power of the Holy Spirit first to get an English-speaking demon to speak to us and then to get it to reveal that its leader was a spirit of control. From experience, I knew that a spirit of control could be a difficult one. I also knew that control demons often impede ministry by controlling much of what goes on. As the demon said when we made contact with him, "I'm in charge." And indeed, he was exerting a lot of control over the situation.

We learned that the spirit had gotten into Julie early in her life. So early, in fact, that she could not remember what it was like not to be under his influence. She had been the oldest daughter in the family of an alcoholic father. This meant that she had to be in charge whenever her mother was not around, which was frequently. To do a good job at taking charge, Julie somehow opened herself up to a demon who helped her but also took a disturbing measure of control over her.

It was the spirit of control that had invited depression and the other demons in. He was very proud of the way he had been able to govern much of Julie's life. Because of his pride and arrogance, then, he volunteered quite a lot of information concerning what he was attached to. As we learned these things, we were able to help Julie to forgive, give Jesus her anger and finally to give up her fear that if the demon left she would no longer have her considerable organizational skills. We also were able to help her give up her very low opinion of herself (a condition we find in most of the women we work with).

By following the clues given us by the demons, then, we were able to accomplish the necessary inner healing and then to cast out the weakened demons. It took several sessions, totaling over fifteen hours but Julie went free, and has continued free for nearly two years. Fifteen hours seems like a lot of time, but it would have taken a lot longer had the demons not provided us with so much information to use against them.

SHOULD WE SEEK INFORMATION FROM DEMONS?

Many believe it is not a good idea to seek information from demons. Their negative counsel seems to stem from four sources. (1) A misuse of verses such as Luke 4:41 where Jesus commanded demons to be silent "because they knew that he was the Messiah." (2) The knowledge that demons can't be trusted, coupled with the fear that when we get information from them, we are not going to be able to prevent ourselves from being misled. (3) A lack of understanding that it is possible to be in control of the situation through the awesome power of the Holy Spirit. It is he, not the demons that is in charge, and he, not we, who is forcing the demons to reveal information that is often against their own best interests. (4) Some reason that by allowing demons to talk through the person, we are giving them more power over the person than they would have had otherwise and, therefore, both allowing demons to use a person they have no right to use and complicating the process of getting them out.

Before I deal specifically with these points, I'd like to make a few general remarks. In a deliverance ministry, we have several ways of finding out essential information. Experience gives us a lot of insight. But with experience we have to be careful lest we fall into the "Moses mistake." He learned once how to get water from a rock, so when God told him to get water again, he stopped listening to how God wanted him to go about it. He simply used the same method that had worked last time. So it is with experience. It is easy to simply do what worked last time without listening to how God wants it done this time. To avoid making that mistake, then, *we attempt to listen to God first.* And he often leads us to draw from what we have learned in other situations.

Frequently, God shows us something quite different from what we have done before. As we ask him to lead us, we get impressions that, if followed, usually turn out to be just the thing he seems to have wanted. So we listen. That's the key.

But as we listen, he often seems to lead us, as he did while we worked with Julie, to use his power to force the demons to give us the information we need to proceed. We are working in the presence and under the power of the Holy Spirit, so we need not be afraid of allowing the Enemy too much power or even of listening to a demon rather than listening to God. It is God who reveals things to us, even through demons! Though we have to be careful (see below), the quickest way to get the insight God wants us to have is often to get it from the demons themselves.

It is important, however, to use information gotten from demons with wisdom and caution. Later in this chapter, I will give both reasons and cautions. But first let's look at the objections:

1. Many assert that Jesus refused to talk to demons. This is not quite accurate. In Mark 1:25, 34; 3:12 and Luke 4:41, Jesus commanded the demons to stop speaking so they would not reveal who he really was. Interestingly, Jesus gave at least some people, including the disciples, the same order (Mk 1:44; Lk 9:21). Jesus insisted on controlling the way and the timing of his self-revelation. He did not allow the demons to have charge of that important part of his mission.

In Mark 5:1-20 and the parallel passage in Luke 8:26-39, Jesus carried on an apparently lengthy conversation with the demons in the Gerasene demoniac. Jesus not only got information from the demons, he allowed them to bargain with him. It is clear, however, that Jesus was in control. He did not allow the demons to take over. In Luke 4:1-13 (and Mt 4:1-11), then, Jesus carried on what probably was a series of conversations with Satan himself.

Those who argue from Jesus' example that we should not talk to demons get no support from Scripture. They do have a point, though. That is, we should not let demons take control of any situation. Often demons will try to distract us by talking or acting in ways that put them in charge. This should not be allowed. Facing demons is a power encounter and we have infinitely more power on our side than they have on theirs. We should use our God-given power to assure that Jesus, not the demons, is in charge.

2. Demons can't be trusted. It is true, demons cannot be trusted. But I'm afraid *the real issue is not whether we can trust demons, but whether we can trust ourselves and God to discern what of the things they say is usable and what will mislead us.* As one who has talked to hundreds of demons, I agree that this is a concern.

However, most of what demons say can be checked out. It can also be controlled. I have frequently told demons to "Shut up!" because they tried to take control away from me and the Holy Spirit. We need to make it clear to them that they are not in control, we (with the Holy Spirit) are. Once I got used to being in control and asserting it, the problem of not trusting the outcome disappeared.

As we grow in listening to God and extracting information from demons, we will find it easy to spot most of their attempts to bluff and distract us. Over and over again, then, in spite of the demons' attempts to mislead, we discover things that enable us to bring inner healing and freedom to our clients more quickly and effectively than otherwise.

A more detailed discussion of the dangers of talking to demons will follow later in this chapter.

3. We should not let the demons be in charge. Though I have touched on this before, a few more words need to be said. Beginners in deliverance ministry often find it difficult to believe that when we turn the ministry session over to the Holy Spirit, he actually does take over. Often it looks like we are simply using natural techniques, so it is easy to be unaware that the Holy Spirit is orchestrating the encounter.

I thought of this just last night while watching a video of our recent deliverance session with the man called Jim I described in an earlier chapter. Skeptics would find little in it to invalidate their skepticism. It looked either like a regular counseling session or as if I were talking to something that wasn't there. The inner healing looked as if it could have taken place in any counsellor's office since the controlling influence of the Holy Spirit, which was suppressing the demons, wasn't visible, except to the "eyes" of those who knew what was truly taking place. But it was this invisible suppression of the demons by the Holy Spirit that made possible the confessions, forgivenesses, and deep healing of Jim.

When I asked the demon whether he could see Jesus and the angels Jesus had assigned to this ministry, I simply looked foolish to those without the eyes to see. Likewise, when I claimed the power of the Holy Spirit to force the demon to state lies he had been feeding Jim over the years. And when the spirit of Rage was made to look at Jesus and he said, "Ooooh, I'm in trouble now!" When the demon swore at me, a skeptic would likely have thought it could be attributed to the normal (though slightly creative) reaction of a hurting person. The skeptic would, however, have a more difficult time explaining the quickness of the dramatic change this client (and his once battered wife) now describe in himself.

It was exciting, however, for me to be reminded through the video of how the Holy Spirit put it all together. First of all, he had been working with Jim before the session. This had opened him up to face his problems, so the session started with his confession of what he had previously denied, that he was a wife-beater. Second, without the suppressing power of the Holy Spirit, I doubt seriously that we would have been able to get so quickly and effectively into Jim's inner wounds. The demons in him were strong ones, perhaps at a level 6 or higher, fully able to interfere with inner healing. Yet it was obvious to me that the Holy Spirit led to keep the session orderly and effective, as one barrier after another was eliminated, until Jim experienced the freedom God wanted for him. A potentially heavy-duty ministry session was completed peacefully (except for the turmoil inside of Jim) and successfully in little more than two hours. Best of all, Jim is brand new.

When the Holy Spirit is in charge, we need not fear the demons, because he is in charge of them too. People often ask me, "How can you be so calm?" It is because I know who is in charge, both of me and the person being ministered to. I also know who I am in Christ.

4. When demons use a person's voice they gain more power. One man vociferously argued that allowing a demon to use a person's voice gave the Enemy even more power. He claimed it would bring permanent damage to the person. He said he would never allow the Enemy that kind of control over anyone he was trying to help.

Though I'm sure that person was sincere, I'm afraid he has the wrong idea of what goes on when, under the power of the Holy Spirit, a demon is forced against his will to do what he already has the power to do (that is, talk to or through the person). But in this case the demon is made to use his normal power to reveal what he wants to hide. He can gain no further power over the person, since he is being weakened through being forced to act against his will. Then he leaves much more gently, with far less trauma to the person, because we have been able to use the information gotten from him to heal the hurts or sins he has been attached to.

Back to Jim. When the strongest demon left, he let out a moderately loud yell. There was a bit of shaking but absolutely nothing that could be classified as violence. And this demon had been pretty powerful, fully capable of considerable violence (which he used frequently against Jim's wife), had we not weakened him before casting him out. Far from leaving some permanent scars on Jim, the possibility of scars was avoided through getting information from the demons that we could use against them. All under the careful control of the Holy Spirit.

LINDA, A PREVIOUS DELIVERANCE BOTCHED

The following story further illustrates the way God works through this valuable ministry tool.

I'll call her Linda. A colleague of mine and I met her during a seminar. Following my teaching on demonization,

Linda approached us for ministry. With desperation in her voice, she told her painful story.

Linda, who had been a national leader in the New Age movement, had become a Christian five years ago. With tears in her eyes, she explained that the last six months had been a constant battle in every area of her life. Among other things, she had been bleeding internally for no medically discernable reason. A greater problem was the constant fear that kept her from almost any activity, including sleep.

Trembling, Linda described her battle with Satan. "I've felt so alone," she began. "Deep down, I know that my problems are due to demonic activity. I've certainly experienced the same feelings during my New Age days. But I've been afraid to get ministry. You see," she said hesitantly, "six months ago, a pastor was praying for me and he identified a demon called Fear. He immediately commanded it to go, and after throwing me down... the demon left. Initially, I felt shaken-up, but relieved that the spirit was gone. But now, I feel certain the demon is back—and my problems are worse than before that deliverance. Please help me. I want to be free once and for all from this spirit—and healed of my bleeding and fears."

Our hearts ached for Linda. We began by asking Jesus to come and bring healing and deliverance. Next, we blessed Linda with peace and invited the Holy Spirit to rest gently upon her. Then we quietly but authoritatively commanded that the spirit of fear be surrounded by the presence of Jesus. We forbade it to hurt Linda, or to embarrass her in any way. We commanded it to tell the truth and said, "In the name of Jesus, if there is a spirit of fear in Linda, we command you to identify yourself." A troubled look came on Linda's face and she said, "A loud voice inside me says, 'What do you want with me?'"

We commanded the demon to tell its name. It replied, "Fear of Failure." After more questioning, We commanded it to say when it entered Linda. Immediately, it replied, "When she was six, at the fire." After these words left Linda's mouth, she looked amazed and then began to cry softly. After a few minutes, she looked up and told us that when she was six, she burned down her father's store. "On that day," she explained, "I was terribly afraid and vowed never again to fail."

We asked Linda to bow her head in prayer as we invited Jesus to take Linda back to that time. Jesus came. Linda vividly pictured Jesus holding her in front of the burning store and pronouncing her forgiven. After that prayer, we commanded the demon to attention and asked if it had additional holds on Linda. Reluctantly, the demon admitted it had none. We then commanded it to leave and go to the feet of Jesus, never to return. Quietly, and with no "show," the demon left Linda.

It's been over a year since that ministry, and Linda continues to be free from fear of failure. She has also experienced freedom from her other fears and from her physical problems. And the information that enabled us to zero in on the problem came from the demon itself!

SOME REASONS IT IS HELPFUL TO GET INFORMATION FROM DEMONS

Ministering to people like Linda is a tremendous blessing. Unfortunately, we encounter many others like her in our ministry, people who have had negative deliverance experiences. More often than not, their deliverances failed because the ministers did not know how to get the information they needed to get the demons out and keep them out.

Getting information from demons is an invaluable tool in helping the wounded. Repeatedly, I have seen God bring his healing and love through our forcing information from demons. Let me share with you six important reasons I believe this practice is a powerful, loving way to bring freedom to the demonized.

1. Much information can be gained that can be used against the demons. Demons when forced to give information by the power of Jesus, will reveal information that is very useful, often critical, in the ministry process. Personally, God shows me more in this way than through words of knowledge. Though words of knowledge and other spiritual gifts are crucial, and we use them freely, this tool is an important adjunct to them.

2. Information from demons can speed healing and lead to deliverance. When deliverance ministers go after demons first, they often do not get to the deeper issues of inner healing, so emotional problems hang on. That approach may take less time than ours, but it usually does not get the whole job done.

Those who focus on inner healing but do not solicit information from the demons may get things done well and quickly, if they are especially gifted in receiving words of knowledge. For most people, however, the combination of words of knowledge and getting information from the demons seems to speed things up.

3. Healing requires information beyond simply knowing a demon is present. Though for some in deliverance ministries the goal is simply to get rid of the demon(s), ours is to bring deep level healing. This requires dealing with the garbage as well as with the rats. And this means we need as much insight into deep level problems as we can get.

God seldom shows through words of knowledge alone all the information deliverance ministers need to heal at the deeper levels. He provides a means for us to learn much more through forcing the demons to admit what they know. Frequently, after we've done the inner healing work and begun to deal with the demons, I've learned there was still something that demons were attached to. One of my favorite questions is, "Does this person have anyone he or she has not yet forgiven?" Time and time again, the answer is, "Yes, so-and-so." Once that person is forgiven, the ballgame is nearly over for the demon(s).

Those who criticize our approach likely are thinking only of getting the demons out, not of the broader healing that is necessary. Even if all we were interested in was the demons, though, the easiest way to find out what other demons are present and who is in charge is to command a demon to reveal that information to us. Before I learned to do this, I found that I frequently cast out lower level demons without finding out what spirit(s) was in charge. By getting them to "squeal" on each other, however, I find it comparatively easy to find out which is the head demon and bind the rest to him in order to throw them all out at once.

4. Forcing demons to give us information weakens them. Since demons work mostly by bluff and deceit, rather than by power, we discover an interesting thing when we force them to give us information against their will. As we demonstrate their weakness by forcing them to obey Jesus, they get upset and discouraged. Many don't seem to have had to face God's power before and seem to think they are invincible. Demons often speak very arrogantly until they begin to feel the power of God directed against them. "This is disgusting!" was the comment of one as he was forced to yield.

One technique I've found useful is to force them to tell me what happened at the cross and the resurrection. Often they will speak freely about the cross, since they believe the myth that Satan was able to defeat Jesus there. But mention of the resurrection gets quite a different response. "I don't want to talk about that," they'll frequently say, or "That's not important." Driving it home to them that their whole kingdom was defeated at the tomb, however, and getting them to admit this truth wears them down. Perhaps, since they are deceivers, they are weakened every time they are forced to speak or to admit the truth. They also seem to be weakened when forced to speak the name of God, Jesus, or the Holy Spirit.

5. Hearing demons confess their lies provides the client with a big boost. Often the person who has heard demonic lies for a long time is not at all sure just what the truth is. To end such confusion, it is useful to force demons to reveal truths about their activities.

Making a demon reveal the lies he has been feeding the person is frequently very helpful. I did this with a lovely older woman I'll call Emily. When I commanded the demon to tell her the lies he'd been feeding her, he came up with this list: She's no good, she's ugly, nobody likes her, it's because she's so undesirable that she's not married, she's a failure in her work, she's never going to reach her goals. As the demon recounted these, the tears came. Emily had been hearing these exact words for years. Now, she knew where they came from. When, then, I forced the demon to tell the truth and he contradicted every one of his original statements, she really got emotional. When I forced him to change "She's ugly," he first admitted, "She's okay." But I pressed him until he spoke the truth, "She's beautiful!" She was (and is) indeed beautiful but this thief had deprived her of her right to accept that truth.

The point is, when we force the truth out of a demon, two things happen: he gets weakened by being forced to obey a greater power, and the person gets strengthened through discovering the truth (from a supernatural source) and learning the origin of the lies. The latter usually relieves guilt and boosts self-image.

Another kind of truth-boost can be illustrated from the experience I had with a woman I'll call Jo. Jo was distraught from a long bout with severe depression. Through counseling, she had come to believe the roots of her depression lay in anger over being sexually abused as a child by her father. She had not, however, been able to remember the event(s). We did a lot of inner healing and then challenged the demons whose influence had become obvious.

Since her story is a common one, I accepted as probable her suspicion that she had been abused and attempted to get the demon to fill in the details her memory would not supply. This wasn't working, however, and, I must confess, I was getting a bit impatient with what I assumed were the demon's diversionary tactics. As is my habit, I was praying silently that God would show me what to do next. All of a sudden, the thought came to me (a potential word of knowledge) that the demon was lying about the abuse, that there had been none at all!

I tested the demon to find out a few additional pieces of information that would make the picture more complete, whichever way it developed. I then took the risk and commanded, "In the name of Jesus Christ I command you to tell us the truth: Was she molested by her father?"

The demon said, "No, she wasn't," admitting that he had held her captive to this lie for years. His power was thus broken, making it easy to get rid of him. It also brought marvelous freedom to Jo from the tangle of hurt coming from suspicion of her father. Knowing (experiencing) the truth (Jn 8:32), even though that truth came from a demon, had made her free.

6. Learning during deliverance to recognize the demon's voice is very helpful after deliverance. When we command a spirit to leave someone, we send it to the feet of Jesus and forbid it ever to return. Though this means they cannot return, often they try to fool people into thinking they have. One person reported that during the night after his deliverance he awoke hearing a voice saying, "We're back!"

Though sleepy, he recognized the voice and mustered enough presence of mind to ask, "Inside or outside?"

They replied, "Outside." So, with a sigh of relief, he commanded them to leave and went back to sleep.

Learning during the deliverance session to recognize both the content and the style of demonic communication equips people to better defend themselves against a demon's deceit after the session is over. The person will be much more aware of which demons were there and how they functioned. Also, the person will be aware of lies and tricks the demon has pulled, and may try to pull again, after hearing the demon speak during the deliverance session(s). Finally, the person will be aware of her/his spiritual authority and how to use it, having seen the deliverance counsellor model how to fight the demon(s).

It's exciting to hear people who have received deliverance describe how they handle demonic attempts to retake territory from which they have been evicted. They say things like, "The demon tried to come back last night, and I did the same thing you did. I told it to leave and it did!" Or, "I asked Jesus to send angels to surround the demon with swords, and they took care of it. And Jesus let me see the whole thing!"

SOME CAUTIONS WHEN GETTING INFORMATION FROM DEMONS

Getting information from demons, then, can be a powerful, effective tool in a deliverance ministry. Hopefully, the above discussion shows that this method is often a most effective and loving way to bring total healing and freedom to the demonized.

Having said this, though, I want to offer some important cautions when working to get information from demons. We need always to be wise and discerning.

Caution 1: Never trust anything a demon says without checking it out. Most demonic information can be checked easily. For example, if a demon tells you it is a generational spirit that entered six generations back on the father's side, that can be checked. When you take authority over that generation and break the demon's power, if it is immediately weaker, it is evident the demon was telling the truth. Or, if a demon states that it entered during a beating at age six, the person usually will affirm the possibility that what the demon said is true. If, after bringing Jesus into that situation through inner healing, the demon can hardly talk, it's a good bet the demon was giving facts.

Most of the information we want from demons is the kind

illustrated in the preceding paragraph. Checking it out is a simple matter of going to the event indicated and letting Jesus repair the damage. Seldom have I found this kind of information from demons to be inaccurate.

When, however, they give more wide-ranging information, they are less trustworthy, especially if they see that by lying they can get you off the track. Some of my colleagues, and occasionally I myself, have questioned demons concerning the organization of the satanic kingdom. Though sometimes they are quite specific, I take it all with great suspicion. Likewise, I regularly ask them to reveal the total number of demons working under a given head demon. They often come up with a very large, suspicious number. But these are incidental matters, seldom important to the task at hand, the healing of the person.

I have found what demons reveal so accurate concerning what needs to be dealt with to weaken their grip, that I tend to trust what they say in this area. I find, furthermore, that they are so consistent in stating, with deep regret, that they cannot live in a Christian's spirit, that I trust them on this. I have quizzed well over a hundred demons on this subject and their answers are the same.

Caution 2: Knowing demons seek to deceive alerts us to command them to tell the truth in the name of Jesus. When soliciting information from demons, always command them to tell the truth in the name of Jesus. Since it is their nature to deceive, don't expect them to tell the truth unless they are commanded to.

When they are confronted with the power of Jesus, they are battling for their lives. It is not an even match. And for many, perhaps most of them, this is the first time they have been confronted with so much power. Often they are completely "freaked out" and don't know what to do. Thus, their response may be more related to their own upset and confusion than to their inability to tell the truth.

How demons can lie even when forbidden to under the

power of the Holy Spirit, I cannot understand. The fact that they tell the truth so often under such a circumstance is, however, surely the result of the Holy Spirit's influence. One thing I've found encouraging, is that very often when they do tell me a lie, the Holy Spirit immediately shows me that it is a lie. I can, therefore, challenge it on the spot and get the truth.

It is important to develop discernment in this area. The benefits are so great, however, that it is worth working at. I have found that the discernment comes with practice and listening to the Holy Spirit. A good rule of thumb is to be skeptical of the demons' responses continually but not to refuse to ask them questions simply because you may be misled occasionally. With prayer, wisdom, and experience, it becomes easier to determine if they are lying.

Caution 3: Deceit is not the same as lying. The myth is abroad that demons always lie. That is definitely not true. Remember that in the temptations of Jesus, it was not lies but the misuse of truth that Satan used (Lk 4:1-13). And remember that the reason Jesus silenced the demons so often was that they recognized him and told the *truth* concerning who he was (Mk 1:24, 34; 3:11; Lk 4:41).

Deceit is a broader concept than lying. And master deceivers like Satan and demons are too smart to lie if they can accomplish their purposes by misusing the truth. They like to deceive by raising questions (as with Adam), or by using truths to bring about an immediate, apparently innocent activity that has long range disastrous consequences (as in Jesus' temptations), or by telling only part of the truth. For example, in pressing a demon to recount the lies he had been feeding a man I was working with, he said, "He's short." This was true but deceiving. For, as I pressed him, the demon confessed that he said that to the person in a derogatory manner, as if there were something wrong with being short.

Deceit is a deliberate attempt to mislead. It is one of the satanic kingdom's primary devices. Watch out for it, even when what the demon is saying is true.

Caution 4: Don't let demons distract or control any part of the ministry. Often demons will try to talk a lot, change the subject, or otherwise attempt to control the session. Don't allow them to do this. It's a power game. Remember, you are the one with more power and you're in control. Make them shut up and only speak when you command them to.

Caution 5: Demons bluff; don't let them scare you. Oftentimes, a demon will try to scare you and your client. Or they will use bluff to get you to leave them alone. They do this in a variety of ways. They may hide behind another demon to make you think they're not there. Or they may use arrogant words or a threatening glare. "She's mine," said one to me recently with about as hateful a look as I've ever seen. Such a show can make the demon appear to be really tough and hard to get out. Knowing demons are mostly bluff, however, I didn't back down. Without batting an eye, I soon had him and his buddies out.

Demons may throw the person around as much as you'll allow. They hope you or the person being ministered to will decide the process is not worth it and stop. Forbidding violence right at the start will usually minimize this problem. If it continues, quietly but firmly keep commanding the demon to stop and go about the inner healing work until it does. Don't give the demon(s) the victory by stopping the session unless it be briefly, to rest or so you can get help from someone with more experience.

Demons also cause pain, call people names, threaten to enter you or members of the deliverance team or to kill you or them, declare they'll never leave, pretend they are a huge principality with more power than you—all to get you "off their backs." On occasion, they'll start recounting your sins or those of someone else on the team. If this happens, simply say, "Those sins are all under the blood, forgiven and forgotten by God. I forbid you to bring them up." Or if these tactics don't work, they may beg for mercy. Several times I've had a demon say something like, "If I promise not to hurt him anymore, will you let me stay?"

But remember who you are and the authority you have in Jesus. Again, it is not an equal contest. You have *infinitely more power* on your side than they do. Command them, in a firm but calm voice, to obey you. Loudness and frantic activity are unnecessary. They help the demons, not Jesus. Let them know whose name you come in and who they are. Remind them that they have been defeated and that the person they are working in belongs to Jesus' kingdom, not to theirs. They are, therefore, trespassing.

The power of Jesus is awesome! And it's exciting to see how quickly the demons have to respond to it, especially once the garbage is taken care of. Before the garbage is worked through, however, the demons have a "legal right" to be there. They can, therefore, often be diversionary until the garbage is cleared away.

Caution 6: There is no sure-fire set of directions as to how best to get information from demons. No two demons are exactly alike. Though they don't seem to differ as much as people do, each has his own personality and behaves in his own way. You, too, will develop your own distinctive style. The interaction between your style, the personal characteristics of the demon(s), and those of the person needing ministry, makes for infinite variety. So don't look for any pat formula for dealing with demons. Continually ask Jesus what to do next and you'll be surprised at what he shows you.

I've learned something each time I minister. Hopefully what my colleagues and I have learned will provide you with enough helpful suggestions to enable you to start or continue your own learning.

THE MOST IMPORTANT POINT

Whatever we learn about technique, we must not lose sight of the most important point in any healing ministry—*there is no substitute for listening to God.* Our greatest weapon is our intimacy with the Father. Learning to listen to him and doing what he wants are both the greatest challenge and the greatest satisfaction I have found. And to be accomplishing things I know I cannot do is incredible but very satisfying; I hope I never have to quit.

Having stressed this essential, I would encourage you to step out in faith to "do the stuff." My experience has shown that *we learn to hear God's voice as we step out in ministry.*

NINE

Getting Demons Out

SEALING THE DEAL

We'll call the demon Owner. He promised to be a strong one. He lived in a six-year-old alter personality (see chapter two, myth 10) of a young woman we'll call Elaine. Her alter, we'll call Edie. Three ministry attempts had been unsuccessful at getting Owner out. Elaine was brought to me by John, who had been ministering to her. They hoped I would know better how to go about getting Edie free and that God would use me to finish the job. Though I had ministered once before to Elaine, I had not met Edie.

Before our appointment, I had alerted several people to be in special prayer. I had also been praying myself and pondering possible approaches God brought to my mind. I did not fast, not because I don't believe in it (see below) but simply because I didn't feel led to. My team consisted of John and myself. It turned out to be crucial that John had good rapport with her. Both Elaine and Edie trusted him very much.

As the session began, Elaine held John's hand, and I prayed what I had been praying all along: that the Holy Spirit would take over, give us the authority and power we needed, plus the insight and guidance necessary to do the job ahead of us. I claimed protection from any revenge on the part of the demons for ourselves and all the people, possessions and other things that pertained to us. I cut off all demons inside Elaine (and Edie) from outside assistance and, again, invited the Holy Spirit to take complete control.

My first task was to establish contact with six-year-old Edie and, if possible, win her trust. As with most alters, the fact that her core person, Elaine, knew and trusted me made little difference to Edie. Elaine had been very badly treated both by her parents and in satanic rituals. Her father had used her sexually countless times and had made her available to other men. Her mother, too, had been very abusive. During an especially abusive sexual experience, this alter, Edie, had split off. So it was difficult for Edie to open up to a man like myself whom she had not known previously.

When I asked Edie questions about herself and her experiences, she kept turning to John, asking him if it was safe to let me know what I had asked. It was pitiful to see and hear how much damage had been done to Edie, but delightful to see the trust she had developed in John. When I felt we had interacted enough for Edie to trust me, I asked permission to make contact with the demon Owner. After getting John's approval, she consented.

"In Jesus' name, I challenge you, Owner" I said. "I command you to come to attention and to respond to me." The demon appeared right away, evidenced by an extremely angry and bothered look on Edie's face. He claimed that he owned her and that neither I nor anyone else was going to take her away from him. He had taken over in that sexual abuse episode when Elaine/Edie had called out to God for help and, apparently, received none. Owner then spoke to the girl, saying that if she allowed him in, he would take away the pain. And Edie, remembering the event, testified that as she let Owner in, he did indeed take away the pain.

Edie then made statements such as, "God did not help me, Owner did," "God is bad, Owner is good," and "Good is bad, bad is good." When I asked Edie if she knew Jesus, she portrayed him as the God who wouldn't help her when she hurt so badly. She portrayed Owner as the one who always came to help her when she needed him. She pleaded, "Why wouldn't Jesus help me?" And I had to confess that I didn't know the answer to that question.

I contended, however, that Jesus both has more power to help than Owner and is more concerned for her good than Owner. This did not square with her interpretation of her experience, though. I added that Owner's real motive was to destroy her—a fact I attempted to get Owner to admit but with only partial success. That is, Owner would admit to wanting her to die, but he contended (and she agreed), death would be much better than the pain she had to live with as a result of the abuse.

The battle was for Edie's will. Both Owner and I knew that all depended on which way she chose to go. If she chose Owner, as she had so often before, he would be the winner. If, however, she chose Jesus, it would be all over for him. So I asked Jesus to assign some large angels to surround Owner, to hinder and weaken him and to cause him pain whenever he did not cooperate. When I asked Owner if he could see the angels, he said he could. He also admitted to seeing Jesus with us in the room.

Next, I got Owner to admit that part of his power came from some curses and dedications put on Elaine/Edie by her father. At this admission, I took authority over those curses and dedications and broke their power in Jesus' name, by the power of his death and resurrection. I then claimed Jesus' freeing power to take Edie's will away from Owner and to heal the hurts she had experienced. I asked Jesus to show himself to Edie in the abusive events. She apparently did not see the latter (as most people are able to do), but perhaps did not completely understand with her six-year-old mind.

In any event, something seemed to happen to Owner's grip on Edie. He still spoke arrogantly. But experience has taught me to listen for the strength in a demon's voice and I could clearly discern a weakening. So I appealed to Edie's will once again, asking her to choose Jesus rather than

Owner. As she considered these options another time, John asked her if she was hearing anything from Owner. "No," she said and, pointing to me, continued, "He told Owner he couldn't talk!" At this point I knew we were winning. Continuing to look at John, the six-year-old asked, "What is Jesus like?"

Hesitating, John gave just the right answer, "He's like me."

"But can he really protect me?" she asked.

"Yes," replied John, "because he has much more power than I do."

So, even though recognizing that it was a risk, since Owner had promised her great pain if she chose Jesus, she chose Jesus. And the pain came. But John said, "In Jesus' name, I bind you Owner and command you to stop causing her pain." And the pain stopped, proving to her that Jesus indeed could stop pain.

Next, I called Owner to attention. Though he had started at perhaps a level 7 or 8 on our scale, now he seemed to be at about a 2 or less. When I asked him if he was ready to go, he simply said, "Okay." So I asked the angels to lower a box over the head of Owner and all other demons over which Owner had authority, and lock them in it. This was done and Owner agreed that he was locked in the box. So I asked the angels to take the locked box to Jesus with Owner safely inside and asked Jesus to dispose of the box and Owner. Edie then was able to picture Jesus crushing the box as if it were in a garbage compactor. Next I said, "I now remove these demons from Edie as far as the East is from the West, and place the cross and empty tomb of Jesus between Edie and the demons. I forbid them ever to come back or ever to send other demons, in the name of Jesus." And it was over; the deal was sealed.

I present this story in some detail because it is a typical ministry session that, though more difficult than most, illustrates many of the points below.

DISCERNING DEMONS

People sometimes ask me, "Do you think I have a demon?" They somehow think I can simply look at them and tell whether or not a demon is in them. I can't. Sorry! Some may have that kind of a gift, but I don't. I can do a bit better if a person describes symptoms for me, but even then I can't be sure. In fact, I hardly ever know until I challenge them in the name of Jesus and get some kind of reaction.

For many, the word "discernment" sounds mystical, especially if it is applied to discerning whether or not a demon is present. Indeed, I used to feel that way myself and wondered if God would ever give me such a gift. It wasn't until I stopped being concerned over whether or not I had discernment, however, that God started using me in a deliverance ministry. When I agreed to follow him rather than to wait for gifting, amazing things began to happen. *We are to seek the Giver, not this or any other gift.*

Since learning to focus solely on Jesus, I've been learning a lot about discernment. For one thing, I've been learning that there are several components to the kind of discernment needed in a deliverance ministry. There is a supernatural component in which God reveals things directly via words of knowledge and wisdom. There is also a natural component made up of experience, ability to observe and interpret, common sense, and imagination.

Since the Holy Spirit will be our guide (after we have asked him to come in a special way), we can expect the process to go well beyond what is possible through merely human abilities. In that sense the whole experience is supernatural. But much of what God uses springs from "natural" capabilities. The natural is combined with the supernatural in discernment, as well as in all other aspects of a deliverance ministry.

Many have the impression that if God really is leading, many spectacular things will happen. Not so. *God seldom does things in a spectacular way. He prefers to do them otherwise.* So when we pray for God to lead in every part of the ministry, we have learned to look for his leading but not to expect a lot of fireworks. Many have missed a lot because they expected God to be more obvious in his leading than he usually chooses to be.

What I call "natural discernment" is by far the most frequent kind of discernment in ministry sessions. Keep your eyes open. Look for any overt manifestations. Often the mere presence of the Holy Spirit flushes demons out and causes them to act strangely. This may happen as the result of simply inviting the Holy Spirit to take over in a ministry session. Or demons may manifest in response to God's presence in worship, personal devotions, or blessings in Jesus' name. I have even seen clear demonic manifestations when I was simply teaching on the topic.

Visible manifestations of demonic presence may also occur in response to challenging demons to manifest themselves. They also may show themselves at other times when the authority of Jesus' name is used, for example, in speaking healing to emotional, spiritual, or physical problems. I've frequently seen them become obvious in one person as a response to challenging demons in another person.

Besides showing overt manifestations, persons inhabited by demons can experience inner disturbances that they are able to hide. Many demonized people regularly have problems, such as headaches or other physical, emotional, or mental problems in church, intended by the demons to undermine their concentration. When I do the back-to-the-womb inner healing procedure as a public exercise, demonized persons regularly experience such hindrances. As one fellow said, "As soon as I started to picture the sperm and the egg, everything went black." His demons didn't like that image one little bit! We worked with him individually, however, and now he's free.

Since any such symptoms can indicate several different things, we need to be careful not to jump too quickly to the conclusion that there is a demon. Among the more common indications of demonic presence are the following: headaches or other pain in the body, lightheadedness, feeling nauseous, stiffness or shaking of the body, unusual sleepiness, a strong desire to strike the counsellor, and a strong desire to run from the session.

Less common manifestations (usually indicating more severe demonization) are: violent shaking, facial or body contortion, screaming, swearing, throwing-up, strange-looking eyes (glazed, squinted or rolled back), "acting out" (as with a homosexual spirit trying to seduce the counsellor), and speaking with another voice.

These are some of the things that can be discerned naturally, either by observation or by asking questions. In addition, God does show things to people supernaturally, though usually in combination with the observation of natural phenomena. As you develop more experience, you will find your ability to discern sharpened. You will also notice that *demons make a lot of mistakes that give them away. Learning to look for these mistakes and to take advantage of them is an important part of the game.*

PREPARATION FOR A DELIVERANCE SESSION

1. A deliverance session should be bathed in prayer. Many find it helpful to fast as well. Though I believe in both, my practice in most situations is to depend on those who pray regularly for me, plus my own praying. Only when I expect the session to be especially challenging (for example, a session following one that has failed), or when I feel impressed by the Lord to do so, do I fast and ask for special prayer. I try to be spiritually ready at all times to do deliverance or to minister to any emotional or physical need.

2. Ministering in teams is best, whenever possible. Though now, after much experience, I frequently minister alone, I like it better when others assist. They bring gifts to the session that I don't have. Even without different gifting, though, they can be praying and listening to the Lord in a way I cannot during the session. My concentration has to be on the person, the problems, and the demons, while theirs can be on listening to God more fully.

A good number for a team is three to five. More than five or six can become confusing. When ministering in a team, one person needs to be in charge. I tell the others they should not break in while I'm leading. I ask them, however, to write on small pieces of paper anything they feel they receive from the Lord and to put those papers on my legs as I minister. God frequently reveals something crucial through those comments.

The choice of people for a team differs from time to time. If the ministry promises to be difficult, I try to get as many experienced members as possible, with as many different giftings as possible. Often, though, one of my objectives is to train people, so I will deliberately gather a mixture of experienced and novices.

It is always important to include those with gifts of discernment. Since, however, discernment is often given situationally by the Holy Spirit, it is likely to be manifested in ministry by anyone with general spiritual sensitivity. When God is leading, natural abilities, experiential insight, words of knowledge, and wisdom all combine to produce supernatural discernment.

3. At the start of each session, take authority over the place, time, and people involved. To take this authority, we use a statement such as: "I speak in Jesus' name against any emissaries of the Evil One who may be here. I command you to leave. I claim this place, this time, these people for the Lord Jesus and forbid any activity by any satanic beings except what I specifically command."

We then pray, asking the Lord for the guidance, authority, and power of the Holy Spirit. Also through prayer, we speak protection over everyone present saying something like, "I claim protection in the name of Jesus Christ for each one of us, our families, our friends, our work associates, our property, our finances, our health, and everything else that pertains to us, from any revenge or other dirty tricks from the Enemy."

Next, it is important to cut off any spirits inside the person from help by other spirits outside or inside the person, saying something like, "In the name of Jesus, I cut off any spirits inside this person from any help they might get from outside spirits or from any others inside the person."

We then forbid any violence, vomiting, or other spectacular behavior as follows: "I forbid any spirits inside this person to cause any violence, any throwing-up, or other showy behavior."

Now we are ready to challenge any demons present.

CHALLENGING DEMONS

Once you are reasonably sure that a demon might be present and inner healing has been brought to a satisfactory point, it is time to challenge the demon(s). By "a satisfactory point," I mean to indicate that at some point in the ministry it becomes a higher priority to deal with the rats that are stirring up the garbage than to deal with the remaining garbage. Usually not all the inner healing the person needs can be done before it is advisable to get rid of the demons. Seldom is it necessary to prolong the inner healing beyond dealing with the most basic issues, since most of the remainder needs to be done independently by the person.

Frequently as we minister inner healing we come to suspect the presence of demons. We often pick up clues that point to influences beyond those of the emotional hurts we have been treating. Though, again, we need to be careful to keep our conclusions tentative, since nearly all symptoms can be simply the result of emotional distress, the following may indicate demonic involvement: compulsive behavior, disturbing dreams, a strong urge toward suicide or murder, intense self-rejection, homosexuality, and occult involvement. If there is serious dysfunction in the family of the person's parental or grandparental families, we may suspect the possibility of an intergenerational spirit or curse. The possibility of other curses, whether self-curses or those imposed by other persons should also be checked out.

1. If we suspect a demon we ask permission to test the possibility. It is good never to go beyond what a person is willing to do. If we ask this permission and the person refuses, we go no further. I let the person know, however, that I'm ready to deal with the problem whenever he or she is. One of my clients let me get well into the process but then jumped up saying, "I don't believe in this stuff!" and stalked out of the room. As he left, I made it clear that I was available if he later chose to continue. Several days later, after the demons had made life difficult for him and, in the process made their presence clear even to him, he called for another appointment. He's now free.

2. I often challenge demons by looking into the person's eyes. If I feel the person might be distracted in some way, though, I suggest closing the eyes for better concentration. With some persons and some demons, eyes open works better. With others it is better to work with the person's eyes shut.

I usually let the person know that I am not certain whether demons are present, but I am going to act as if there are, to see if I can rouse one. Since demons don't like to be discovered, they need to be challenged. I've found a direct challenge is best, even if I'm not sure one is there.

I usually try to challenge the demon using whatever names of emotional or spiritual problems I suspect are being reinforced by demons. Typically, I'll say something like, "Spirit of _____, I challenge you in the name of Jesus Christ. I command you to come to attention."

Usually I have to challenge one or more spirits several times before I get a response. Often I add, "I forbid you to hide." Not infrequently, it is necessary to challenge several demons before you get a response from any. I often try several names in succession, which requires patience and persistence. I'll frequently press hardest on those I think may be weakest on the assumption that they may be easier to get to respond than the stronger ones.

If I don't have an idea of what the spirit's name might be, I command it to tell me what it is. Getting them to admit their names is often difficult. Expect words of knowledge at this point. Follow up any hunch. Or simply call for "Head Spirit" to come to attention. Sometimes the spirit has already done something by which it can be identified. For example, "Spirit that has caused that shaking, come to attention."

The spirit may try to keep the person from maintaining eye contact, a typical diversionary tactic. If the demon does this, order it to look at you. Keep control. Don't permit this or any other diversionary tactic such as causing pain, shaking the person, bringing distracting thoughts to the person's mind, telling the person lies (such as, "Demons don't exist"). *Forbid them to exert any control at all.* You don't need to shout or resort to strange things, like placing a Bible on the person's head. This is a power game. Demons respond only to the power exerted over them. And that power is wielded through Holy Spirit-empowered words.

3. Ask Jesus for powerful angels to assist. Often, then, I ask the demon if he can see the angels. I also ask if he can see Jesus here with us. Usually they admit that they can see both the angels and Jesus. Or they'll mention they are very uncomfortable in their presence. This is a good sign. It intimidates them and establishes who's in charge.

4. Next, I try to discover what the hierarchy of spirits is. That is, I try to get whatever demon I contact to tell me who is over him. Sometimes I bluff them into "ratting" on fellow demons by guessing that those tending to appear at the top are present (see chapter six). This tactic, plus words of knowledge, usually leads us to the one(s) on top. *When I find who's the leader, I bind all his underlings to him, so I can deal with all of them at once.* This saves a lot of work when, as usual, there are many demons on hand.

As mentioned in chapter six, demons cluster in groups with one acting as head. Sometimes more than one group is in a person, with head demons of approximately equal authority. When I find this, I bind each group to its head thusly: "By the authority of the Holy Spirit, I tie you all together with… [name the head spirit]."

I then make sure this binding together has actually happened by quizzing the head demon about whether or not all of them are bound to him. Often he will indicate that some are not. I command him to give me the reason. "Do they still have anything on so-and-so?" I will frequently ask. Either the head demon or one of those not bound will then, when commanded, tell me what still needs work. Dealing with the remaining issues usually weakens the wandering demons to the point where they join the bound ones.

GO FOR INTERGENERATIONAL SPIRITS OR CURSES FIRST

Force the demon to tell you if he has any grip through inheritance. You already may have discovered that to be the case during the back-to-the-womb procedure and cleaned up any problem due to inheritance. To be sure, however, I will often say, "In the name of Jesus I command you to tell me if you have any grip through inheritance."

If there is something ask, "Through your mother or father?" and then, "How many generations back?"

If there is an intergenerational root, I say something like the following: "In the name of Jesus I take authority over that ancestor six generations back and break your power in the sixth, fifth, fourth, third, and second generations. Now I break your power over [person's name] father/mother and cut off any power you have over her/him through your involvement in this family at the point of _____'s conception."

We often see a noticeable change in the strength of the demon after this is done. As I have said earlier, I don't know whether what is inherited is the demon itself or some power to which the demon is able to connect. This approach, however, usually brings some release to the person and weakens the demon.

If you suspect an intergenerational root but for some reason can't get confirmation either by word of knowledge or from the demon, guess that there may be one and say something like, "In the name of Jesus, I take authority over the intergenerational spirit of [depression] coming through the father's bloodline and break your power in Jesus' name. I forbid you to have any more power over [person's name]." Or, you could say, "I break the power of the curse concerning [homosexuality] that has come through the mother's bloodline in the name of Jesus Christ."

Though it's good to be right on the mark, the vagaries of what we're doing are such that we're not always sure what is happening. If in doubt, I believe it's better to break the power of a curse or intergenerational spirit that's not there than to miss one that is there! In any event, the ability of inherited weaknesses to empower demons seems great. Breaking any power stemming from ancestry can have a major effect on the strength of the person's demons.

GETTING COMPLETELY RID OF DEMONS

By now, most of the demons' power should be gone as the result of inner healing and the breaking of intergenerational ties. However, some things may remain hidden, so don't be upset if the demons aren't quite ready to go.

I frequently ask the head demon if he is ready to go or if he and his underlings still have anything on the person. They usually will claim nothing is left, even if there is. Often, either because they admit there is still something there or because they refuse to leave, you will need to return to the inner healing mode and deal with additional garbage.

You should *feel free to interrupt the process at any time* to take care of whatever arises. There is nothing magical about the continuity of any part of the ministry. Frequently, it is advisable to take a break to discuss strategy with your team. If you do, I suggest you say to the spirit world, "In the name of Jesus, I forbid the spirit world to hear what we are about to say." It works! Other things worth interrupting the session for are to stretch, go to the bathroom, to pray for more guidance and power, and to call for additional team members.

When you are ready, take authority and command the head spirit with all of its followers to leave. As at all other times, commands should be firm and forceful but not loud. Demons aren't hard of hearing (though I've found it sometimes helps them to hear and obey if I anoint the person's ears with oil that has been blessed). Jesus did not coax out demons as did the Pharisees of his day. He treated them roughly. He *cast* (*ekballo*) them out (Mk 1:25). Be forceful, authoritative, and determined, even as you are patient.

There are several ways to get the demons out. Sometimes you can simply say, "Spirit of _____, I command you to leave/come out in Jesus' name and to go to the feet of Jesus."

If they leave, well and good. Usually, however, this is not enough. If the head demon refuses, command it to tell you what right/grounds it still has to live in the person. Command it in the name of Jesus to tell the complete truth. You may find it useful to remind the demon again who he is, and how he and his kingdom have been defeated. Remind him of the cross and the empty tomb. Demons don't like to hear about the blood shed on the cross or the tomb from which Jesus escaped.

What seems to work best for me in sealing the deal is to ask Jesus if he will have the angels lower a box or bag over the tied-together demons and lock them in, so they are all together and none can escape. I then check with the head demon to see if all are locked in. When they are, I ask the angels to take them to Jesus. The person can usually see this happening. Then I ask Jesus to dispose of the box/bag and separate the demons from the person forever. The person usually sees what Jesus does with the box/bag.

When Jesus has disposed of it, I say something like, "I separate the demons from [person's name] as far as the East is from the West and place the cross on which Jesus died and the tomb from which he rose again between [person's name] and these demons forever. I forbid any of these demons to ever return or to send any others."

That usually does it. If not, look for more garbage and deal with it through inner healing. Then do these steps again.

Important in a deliverance ministry is to keep the sessions to a reasonable length. Though I have gone as long as eleven (!) hours in a single session, I don't recommend it. The best length (for me, at least) is two and a half to three hours. If it lasts longer, fatigue may become a major factor for both the ones ministering and the one ministered to. When people are tired, the Enemy may gain an advantage he wouldn't have otherwise.

If you have worked long enough but more remains, simply shut the demons down by commanding them not to cause the person any harm "until the next time they are challenged in the name of Jesus." This makes it possible for another person challenging them in Jesus' name to have access to them. One person told me she shut them down "until *she* called them up again," only to find that another person who had an opportunity to minister to her client between sessions could not get the demons to respond.

TACTICS—THEIRS AND OURS

Demons regularly use certain tactics to keep from having to leave. We need to know what to do about such tactics. Demonic ruses include:

1. Demons like to delude you about their presence. When you perceive or guess that demons are hiding, simply forbid them to continue. Command the demon you want to respond to you. If this doesn't work, force another demon to tell you what the one you want is doing and if he is still there. This will usually flush him out. If not, do other things and come back later. As the more powerful ones get weakened, they have less ability to resist such orders.

2. Demons sometimes will respond one after another to confuse you. If this happens, you'll quickly discover it. Simply command the one you want by name and forbid him to allow another to talk until you address that other one. You are in charge. Don't let them take control.

3. Demons often talk big to get you to fear them. Demons seldom are as big or powerful as they contend, even if they cause weird facial expressions, pain, and bodily distortions. Sometimes they'll tell you, "I'm a principality" or even "I'm Satan," in hopes you will fear them. Don't give in to them. You have more power than they do. When you call their bluff and remind them who they are and who you are, they get in line.

4. Demons will deceive and lie. As pointed out in chapter eight, take everything demons say with a grain of salt. Order them to tell the truth but still don't trust them. Always be on your guard against their attempts to mislead you and to get you to leave them alone. Often I've had demons say to me, "I'm leaving now" or "I'm gone." Don't believe statements like those. Keep pressing until the deal is sealed.

5. Demons often give excuses and even plead to be allowed to stay. "This is my home. Where would I go?" they say, or "I only help her," or "If I promise not to hurt him, will you let me stay?" or simply "I don't want to leave." I've even had them tell me when things got tough for them, "That's not fair!" When they say that, I usually ask if they've been fair to the person. One replied, "But that's different. We're demons. You're a Christian. You're supposed to be fair!" He got an "A" for creativity, but got no concessions from me.

One of the "bargains" some inexperienced people have fallen for is the request to be allowed to enter someone else. Don't allow it. If they threaten to enter someone, either a team member or someone not there, simply forbid that to happen and it cannot. Claim protection for the person in the name of Jesus and the person is safe. Or, remind the demon that the group is already protected (in the opening prayer) and thus, he has no power to attack anyone.

Don't fall for any such bargaining. Demons are evil beings. They don't play fair. Nor do they keep any promises. No matter how sincere their pleas sound, or how much they try to play on your sympathies, don't weaken.

6. Demons will try to wear you and the person down. Demons use fatigue in any way they can, so don't let sessions get too long. Take breaks from time to time. They also will try to get the person to feel tired even if he is not in fact. They may try to put the person to sleep. All these tactics are designed to discourage and weaken the will of both the demonized person and the counsellor. Carefully watch and protect against them.

If demons won't come out no matter what you do, don't get discouraged. Schedule further sessions and arrange for more experienced people to be on the ministry team (as John did in the story at the beginning of this chapter). Get others praying for the sessions, pray and fast yourself before the next session, and patiently but persistently keep working to free the person.

In addition, it is good to give the person "homework" to do between sessions. This should include prayer and worship (private and public), Bible study, dealing independently with unfinished inner healing, and even encouraging persons to challenge demon(s) themselves. Encourage will-strengthening activities such as small support groups, memorizing and claiming biblical promises, plus constantly playing and singing praise songs.

If deliverance is in God's timing, and the person's will is

properly engaged, most attempts to free a person will eventually be successful. If, consciously or unconsciously, the person does not want to be freed, it is very unlikely that it will happen. God seldom overrides a person's free will—unless, of course, others band together in prayer to bring it about, as in the account of Elizabeth in chapter six. An important caution needs to be made here: Even if you suspect the person doesn't want to exercise his or her will to be freed, never accuse the person of this. Since we can't know for sure, love requires that rather than accuse the person, we patiently attempt to lead the person to want to be freed.

7. The person usually knows when the demons leave. The person usually has a sizeable feeling of relief, as if a great weight has been removed. Sometimes such freedom is so unfamiliar that the person will remark that it feels very strange. I have mentioned this earlier.

Frequently, the person will feel the demons leave through an orifice—the mouth (possibly accompanied by a burp, yawn, or shout), nose, eyes, ears, anus, or vagina. When it is obvious that a demon is located at or near an orifice, sometimes it is appropriate to command them to leave in this way. Often though, they will try to deceive you into thinking they've left by causing the person to yawn, burp, or shout. Sometimes shaking of the body will be followed by release. Or, if the demon has a grip on some part of the body (e.g., head, throat), the person will feel the release of that grip. Such feelings of release can result from the demons leaving or can be an attempt to deceive. Check them carefully by commanding the demon(s) to speak again. Do this several times until you and your client are convinced they have actually left.

When the demons are commanded to get into a locked box, the feeling they are leaving through an orifice doesn't occur. The person will, however, often feel a definite release in the body and be certain of freedom. This release may or may not be noticed right away, however, due to the intensity of the activity of getting them out. Often, the person is intent on watching Jesus deal with the box as the demons leave and then on receiving a hug from Jesus. Only after that picturing does the person physically sense release.

8. Fill the space emptied of demons with blessings. As we usually do in inner healing, we like to bless the person with freedom in the area(s) in which the demon(s) held the person in bondage. For example, if the demon was a spirit of fear, bless with peace and hope; if a spirit of anger, bless with patience and forgiveness; if a spirit of self-rejection, bless with self-acceptance and love.

POST-DELIVERANCE COUNSELING

It is important to counsel the newly-freed person about what is likely to happen after deliverance and how to handle it. Before concluding the ministry session, be sure to forbid the demons to return. If you forget, they may be able to come back. I like to use words such as the following: "In Jesus' name we forbid any of these spirits or any others to return. We declare that this person belongs totally to Jesus Christ and allow no further trespassing by Enemy agents."

I then like to "seal" all that the Holy Spirit has done by saying, "I seal in Jesus' name all that he has done here. We close all doors through which the demons gained entrance and remove all vulnerabilities in Jesus' name."

Demons often try to come back to reclaim their former territory. They will try, but if they have been forbidden, they cannot. The person should know this. But demons can try to fake it by working from outside the person, if allowed. The person should, therefore, be instructed to use the power he has in Christ to forbid them to do anything more.

Let the person know that every believer has the same Holy Spirit as the one who ministered and, therefore, the same authority. James 4:7 says, "Resist the devil and he will flee from you" (NIV). Each delivered person is, therefore, to take authority over any demons that try to return and to send them away again. Eventually they will get tired of trying and go somewhere else. If the demons don't give up right away, neither should we.

We should strongly remind delivered people of who they are in Christ. The Enemy has been lying to them about this, for he doesn't want us to know who we are. Freed people need to assert their will in a new way to make the truth theirs. Believers are Jesus' children (Rom 8:14-17; 1 Jn 3:1-3; Gal 4:5-7), set apart to become like Jesus (Rom 8:29), called by Jesus his "friends" (Jn 15:15). Jesus himself chose them (Jn 15:16) and empowered them (Lk 9:1). Any fear they feel is to be banished since fear is not from God (2 Tm 1:7).

The person will need to get into a support group and begin working with a professional Christian counsellor. Healing requires both therapy and support. Often the best arrangement is for part or all of the ministry team to continue as a support group. Close interrelationships with other Christians can help ward off most of what the Enemy brings to us. Enfolding into a church and Sunday School class can be ideal. Beyond the value of fellowship, such a group can also advise if the person needs more therapy.

It is very important for freed ones to keep clean of whatever the demons attached themselves to. They must will to change habits, attitudes, friends, whatever may be necessary to keep and build on the healing and freedom God has given. Returning to old patterns can open the door for further infestation. For example, a woman I was working with out of whom we cast a spirit of death, tried suicide again and another spirit of death entered her. The person probably needs to work at getting healed in related areas not yet dealt with, lest they afford opportunity for demons to reenter. Personal spiritual growth is needed. Prayer, praise, worship, and devotions are all a part of that growth.

NOW GO AND DO THE STUFF

Now that you know how to release people from demons, try it. It's risky, but anything we do with God is a risk. That's what faith is all about.

Just keep the following in mind:

1. Maintain the person's dignity at all times. Do your best to keep the person from being hurt or embarrassed. Forbid the demons to cause violence, vomiting, pain, or any other discomfort. Also, don't make people confess or openly express anything they would rather hide. Allow them to deal directly with God alone. In addition, be careful and tentative with what you think are words of knowledge. Not all of them are to be shared. Some are for your benefit only (for example, "She doesn't want to be healed"). If anything is not loving, it's not to be said or done because it isn't from Jesus.

2. It is loving to weaken the demons through inner healing before and during deliverance. Don't neglect the garbage. When the demons are thus weakened, they can't do much. So, out of love for the client, weaken them before attempting to cast them out.

3. Before each session, have others (especially intercessors) praying for you. You pray also. And if you suspect the deliverance will be tough, both they and you should fast. Have them join you in praying protection for self, family, and friends of both the counsellor and the person being delivered.

4. Cleanse the room of all evil spirits before starting a deliverance session. Command all spirits that are not of God to leave the room in the name of Jesus Christ.

5. Strengthen the person's will at every opportunity. There are three keys to deliverance: God's power, the person's will, and getting rid of the garbage the demons cling to in the person. Demons will do their best to weaken the person's will because they know they cannot stand against a human will that's set against them. To weaken a will demons frequently use bluff, fear, and fatigue. Both while inside and even after they are out, they will try to bluff the person into thinking nothing has changed. Often they'll bring back similar symptoms, even from outside of the person. They'll also use fear, both during and after the session. Often they'll threaten such things as violence, accident, and revenge through attack on the person or relatives. In addition, they'll use fatigue, both during and after the session to discourage the person. Patiently encourage and strengthen the person against such will-weakeners.

6. Continually encourage the person during and after the session. This helps the person gain strength of will. Tell stories of previous victories that the person can identify with. Demonstrate God's power over the demons during the session by doing such things as blessing and forbidding the demons to do things. Assure the person that he or she possesses the same power, and even allow the person to try it out during the session. Encourage, encourage, encourage.

7. Anointing oil that has been blessed may help. I've found that some demons show no response to the use of oil while others seem to be freaked out by it. It is worth experimenting with. But don't use oil until you have empowered it by invoking Jesus' name over it in blessing.

8. Cleanse buildings and objects infested with enemy power. The person's home may be inhabited by evil spirits. If so, go through it room by room and break any evil power by sending away the spirits and inviting the Holy Spirit to take over. Anointing oil may be used to seal each room. I usually use it to make the sign of the cross above each doorway.

In addition, objects in the home (for example, from overseas) or worn by the person (for example, jewelry) may contain evil spirits. Pray for God to lead you to them. Cleanse them by breaking the evil power in them and then bless them with God's power, or destroy them.

TEN

Twists and Turns in Deliverance Ministry

But when he, the Spirit of truth, comes, he will guide you into all truth. He will not speak on his own; he will speak only what he hears, and he will tell you what is yet to come. Jn 16:13, NIV

"Not by might nor by power, but by my spirit," says the Lord Almighty. Zec 4:6, NIV

Let us keep our eyes fixed on Jesus. Heb 12:2

DOING WHAT WE KNOW WE CAN'T DO

I cannot get over the fact that God has given us the inestimable privilege of working together with him to do what would otherwise be impossible. *I* cannot cast a demon out. *I* cannot know things that don't come from my own intelligence or experience. The works I have been talking about in this book are beyond what ordinary human beings can do. And yet they are happening in my experience weekly. In the last two days, I have had two of these fantastic experiences. One is the lead-in story for chapter nine.

How can this be? Only because God wants us to share in his joy at bringing freedom to people. And only because he deigns to use his power through powerless people like you and me. It's hard to believe, especially for someone like me, who has struggled with self-rejection. But I can't deny it. It happens too often!

Here we see the impossible done in the life of a woman I'll call Ginny.

All of us could feel the darkness and oppression when the plane landed. At the urgent request of missionaries, we had come for a ten day seminar on spiritual warfare in Africa. Many missionaries were reported to be leaving the country due to severe depression and fear.

We met Ginny the first day. Immediately, it was apparent she was an angry young woman. Since her arrival six months earlier, Ginny had become paralyzed by fear and a deep mistrust of everyone. Ginny told us in no uncertain terms that she didn't need ministry and wanted us to leave. After several days, however, she began to soften. Finally, she agreed to let two women on my ministry team pray for her. They recount the following story from their time together.

When they sat down to pray together, Ginny admitted she was terrified of demons. With obvious pain, she confessed that she desperately wanted to trust God, but didn't believe he really loved her. Her experience as a Christian had provided her with a solid, intellectual understanding of the biblical truth that Jesus loved her. Deep within, however, she felt abandoned. In fact, Ginny described her relationship with Jesus like that of a wounded child trying to reach out to a faraway God. Consequently, deep-seated fear and mistrust were ruling her life. These problems had become so extreme that if her husband left her side even momentarily, panic and rage overcame her.

The leader began the ministry by asking Jesus to come and quiet Ginny with his love. They prayed that Jesus would fill her with his light and wrap her in a security blanket of his love and peace. Soon, the lines of tension on Ginny's face softened as the Holy Spirit rested gently on her. Then an amazing thing took place. The one praying stopped and said, "I'm getting a very strong impression, Ginny, that I believe may be from God. As I am listening for the voice of Jesus, I keep hearing him say, 'Tell Ginny this: Jesus is jealous. Tell her that I am jealous for her and long to hold her, to comfort her, to draw her back to me. I am here, and I want to restore an intimate relationship with her.'"

Hearing that, Ginny burst into tears and for several minutes cried softly. Finally, she looked up with tears running down her face and prayed to Jesus, "I'm so sorry, Lord. Thank you that you care enough to be jealous over me. Thank you that you're really here and that you do love me." They then asked Jesus to overwhelm Ginny with his love, dispel her fear, and to restore her trust in his protection and love. Jesus did above and beyond what they prayed. Ginny looked up, a radiant smile broke out on her face, and she began laughing while her husband stared in amazement! The ministry team looked at each other with a combination of confusion and joy. Finally, Ginny was able to stop laughing and share what was happening to her.

"When you prayed for him to come and help me trust him, I felt strong, loving arms circle around me. For the first time in my life, I felt so very safe. It was wonderful! And then, do you know what he did? He began to give me presents... flowers, and toys, and beautiful packages. It was just like birthdays I always dreamed of, but my family couldn't afford. I never dreamed that he loved me this much. I just never really understood that he was this close, longing to protect me and love me."

That late spring night, Ginny's life was changed. In fact, her husband told us she woke up the next day laughing and singing praises to God! Her children were overwhelmed with joy and kept asking their father, "Dad, we've never even seen Mom smile, let alone laugh before. What happened last night?" Although their father couldn't completely explain this dramatic change in their mother, one thing seemed certain: Jesus had touched Ginny in a deep way that not only freed her from demonization but changed her view of Father God, giving her new freedom and hope.

Time and again, we see Jesus touch people in ways they never dreamed possible. Our gracious God always seems willing to speak that healing word when we enter his presence and listen. In Ginny's case, this intimate touch of Jesus broke through her intellectual understanding of his love and allowed her to *experience* his loving her. That life-changing touch by the Holy Spirit is one example of what we call *intimacy with Jesus*. When Jesus restored trust and a deeper intimacy within Ginny, she gained the most powerful weapon available to fight against the powers of darkness.

After Ginny truly knew how precious she was to Jesus, the battle was really over. Several demons were discovered in her during the ministry session. But the most significant problem for Ginny was not the demons, but her damaged relationship with Jesus. Once her intimacy with him was restored through his supernatural touch, the demons of fear and mistrust were quickly defeated by the perfect love of Jesus.

The first "twist, turn, and question," then, is the mystery of how God does such things in a person's life and how he lets us participate. But there are other, more mundane ones as well.

TWISTS AND TURNS

What I mean by twists and turns is that a lot of very unexpected things happen as we minister to the demonized. Among them are the following:

1. Though there is a demon, the person may not allow him to respond. Unless the demon is very powerful, it needs to receive permission from the host person to use his or her vocal apparatus. I suspect withholding permission can be either conscious or unconscious. This problem usually arises with a person who is frightened of the process and fearful of being embarrassed. When we suspect this is the reason, we do two things.

First, we explain that the ministry session is not only under the control of the one leading, but that of the person being ministered to. The latter can at anytime either grant or retract permission for the demon to do things. So can the person leading. Having explained this, we again ask the person to grant the demon permission to interact with us.

This happened with a man I'll call Rick. It was evident he was experiencing demonic interference. There were strong physical manifestations when demons were addressed, including crossing of his eyes and shaking. I forbade these and they stopped. But these symptoms so frightened Rick that he quite consciously withheld his permission for them to speak, even though he had come voluntarily and wanted badly to be free. But the demons had convinced him that if he allowed them to obey me and to speak, they would overpower him and embarrass him in front of the people who were watching. So we briefly discussed our power as believers over demons and he accepted the truth that they were not as strong as they claimed. He then gave permission, and the deliverance proceeded smoothly and successfully.

2. There are several other reasons why demons don't give the information we want. Among them is the fact that a weaker spirit may fear retaliation from those above him. More powerful demons apparently can take it out on underlings who displease them. On occasion, in order to get the help I wanted, I have forbidden the stronger demons to retaliate. I have even spoken a "hedge of protection" around the lesser demon to protect it from revenge. Though demons work together, there is little harmony in the satanic kingdom. They are not, necessarily, loyal to each other. The fact that they are more concerned with their own best interests than with their cause can be used to pit one against another.

One of my colleagues had identified a spirit of pain in a woman we'll call Nancy. As he tried to get information from the spirit, it complained that other demons were attacking it. When they were forbidden to attack Pain, it was able to supply the information needed.

Another reason demons may not respond is that they genuinely may not know the answer to the question we're asking. I often ask demons to tell me how many of them are there. Frequently, they don't seem to know. Though their knowledge can be impressive, they are not omniscient. They cannot, therefore, know the future. Ordinarily, they do not know anything about the person's life before they got in. They can, however, usually reveal when and how they got in and what they've been doing to gain advantage over their host.

3. A weakened head demon may no longer be able to control those under him. This happened from time to time before I learned I should bind all the demons together early in the session. Previously, I had assumed that once the strongest demon was weakened, so would the lesser demons be. I also used to bind them together by commanding the head demon to join the others to him, rather than giving the order myself. This often did not work if the strongest demon was so reduced in power that he no longer could control the others. This meant each of them had to be handled individually.

Now I quite early command them all to be bound to the head demon by the power of the Holy Spirit. Then I am able to deal with all of the demons together. A lower level demon may turn out to have more power than the head at some point during the session. Since, however, they are already bound together, this doesn't complicate the process. It simply means we have to deal separately with the garbage to which that lower-level demon is attached to weaken him to the level of the others.

To illustrate, in several cases I have been able to establish that a demon of death headed the group. However, spirits of fear and rejection seemed to have a stronger grip on the person. The reason seemed to be that the person had been more successful in preventing the spirit of death from doing his work than in preventing the others. Perhaps one explanation was that being pushed toward suicide (as the spirit of death had been attempting) was more obvious and, therefore, easier to resist than the pushes toward fear and rejection. Whatever the reason, I first bound them all together with their head (Death) and then found out from Death, Fear, and Rejection what inner healing needed to be done. Using this information, then, I was able to take away all that gave the lesser spirits their power and then to banish them all.

4. Once demons are bound, many lesser demons will defect if given permission. When I bind the demons together, I have learned to speak to the lesser demons as follows: "I give the demons under the spirit of [name of head demon] two options. You may wait until [name of head demon] leaves and go with him. Or you may defect at any time. But once you leave, you can never come back."

What happens is often very interesting. Sometimes, a lot of them defect immediately, since the garbage they were attached to is gone. And, as the inner healing continues to take away more garbage, others defect also. I commanded one head demon to tell me how many he had under him. He said three hundred and eighty-six, though I didn't believe that number. I then gave the underlings permission to defect and, in response to my successive requests for the numbers during the session, he said "three hundred and eighty-five, the traitor!," "two hundred and fifty-four," "one hundred and thirty-two," "double digits" and "pick a number between one and fifty!" Even though the numbers were probably exaggerated, it was obvious that the head demon was losing his power, and also that he had a sense of humor. And he was soon gone too.

5. Demons may leave parts of them behind. I have no idea how this works or if I'm being deceived in this observation. What I can report, however, is that on several occasions something like the following has happened. We had worked hard to get a spirit of Freemasonry (and many others) out of Lori (see page 130). After we thought that the spirit had left, I asked another spirit if Freemasonry had left. His reply was, "Most of him." Though Lori had not participated in Freemasonry (Rainbow Girls) for about twenty years, her name was still on their books. So I advised her to write a letter renouncing her membership and see that her name was removed from their records. During the next session we had with Lori, I asked a demon if that part of Freemasonry was still there. He said simply, "No. The letter." Because Lori had written the letter renouncing her membership in Freemasonry, the rest of the demon had to leave.

Ellen Kearney, a colleague of mine, reports that in ministering to a man we'll call Jason, her team had been able to get him delivered of a demon presenting itself as a tiger. The demon was cast out when Jason was willing to give up the idea that it helped him to deal with his emotional problems. Some weeks later, however, it was discovered that, though the tiger demon was mostly gone, part of it was left, "the tail." They found that Jason was still putting some trust in the demon for help. When that was dealt with and given up, then, the tail of the demon left also.

I have learned to command that "Every bit of every demon" be combined with the head demon. I often add, "I want no pieces of any of you to remain." This seems to take care of the problem.

6. Deliverance may need to precede inner healing. We have established that the main issue in ministry is dealing with the emotional garbage and that the demons are secondary. Deep-level healing is, therefore, our priority. There are times, however, when demons so interfere with the inner healing process that it is virtually impossible to do meaningful inner healing, so we go after them first. This is not a bad option as long as the person is open to it. Sometimes it can shorten things considerably, since the demons can be made to tell us what deep-level healing needs to be done.

In such a case, I often call up the demon and command him to tell me what he and the others are "hooked" to. I'll ask about intergenerational concerns and the demon will tell me if there are any. If so, we break their power. Then I go back to the demon for more information, perhaps about pre-natal and childhood events that allowed the demons their grip. When they admit to something, we simply go to the person and deal with it in order to take it away from the demons. In this way we get the work done, often quite efficiently. We also can get a good reading on our effectiveness by noting the diminishing strength of the demon's voice.

7. We can forbid demons to hear what is being said. A woman I'll name Bea called me on a Wednesday. As she began to describe her problems, I said something like, "In Jesus' name I speak confusion to the Enemy's communication system and forbid any members of that kingdom to hear what we're talking about or to interfere in our plans in any way."

On the following Saturday, as I was ministering to Bea, I asked the head demon, a spirit of death, if he knew I was coming. He said, "No. She knew but wouldn't tell us." I then asked if he had been able to get information from the spirits in the Pasadena area where I live and work. He replied, "I couldn't. You put a hedge around me."

It is interesting and reassuring to know we have this kind of authority. It is useful to forbid evil spirits to hear when we are making plans. Just as demons can be commanded to answer questions and forbidden to act, so they can be stopped from hearing conversations. I find it a good idea to stop at various points during a ministry session to assess where we are and explain to the person what is happening. It is good at these times to prevent evil spirits from hearing our analysis and strategy. I simply say, "I forbid any representatives of the Enemy's kingdom to hear what we're about to say." When we return to talking to the demons again, though, *it is important to release them from their deafness.* Otherwise, they may not be able to hear when we speak to them. We can simply say, "Spirit of [name of demon] I permit you to hear again."

8. Demons may attack members of the ministry team. As the leader's attention is on the person receiving ministry, Enemy forces may find someone in the group that is vulnerable and attack that person. This is one way demons attempt to distract the attention of the team from the job at hand. Often this will occur in the form of a physical pain or sensation. Or people may sense an oppressive feeling in the room. The problem can usually be stopped by rebuking the spirit behind the attack or, in the case of a room that feels oppressive, by praying over it to cleanse it.

Such an attack occurred recently when a team member I'll call Shari received a word of knowledge concerning the need to break a curse. As Shari rose to lay hands on the person receiving ministry, she experienced a sharp pain in her leg and nearly fell because of it. Understanding that this can happen, Shari simply rebuked the spirit causing the pain and it left immediately.

9. Spirits can be shared with others. Sometimes during ministry we have lost contact with a demon and couldn't figure out what happened until we got onto the concept of what are called "shared spirits." A shared spirit is one that lives in more than one person. It can flip back and forth between the people and, therefore, when identified in a deliverance session, has somewhere else to go to to avoid the pressure. The late Ernest Rockstad, in relating one of his experiences with a shared spirit, spoke of how the spirit traveled to the woman's mother over five hundred miles away. But it appeared immediately again in the one he was counseling when commanded to. It claimed to be able to travel "at the speed of thought."

I once worked with a husband and wife who shared a spirit of death. I commanded it to be in the husband completely and forbade it to move back and forth. Later, when working with the wife, I asked another demon if that spirit was still in her. "No," he said, "he's in a box somewhere!"

Usually it is family members or those with extremely close relationships that will share a spirit. Since demons cannot be in two places at the same time, though, they will be in one or the other at any given moment. This raises the possibility that if a demon is temporarily gone from the person being delivered, it will not be cast out with the rest. It can, therefore, return later and continue its residence there. It is good to anticipate the possibility of shared spirits, especially if you are working with one spouse and suspect the other is also demonized. If you suspect shared spirits, simply command all of them to be in the one you are dealing with and forbid them to go anywhere else until commanded to leave. The demonic world has a highly developed communication system and any such spirits will hear and respond quickly. When you expel the spirits, then, be sure to forbid them access to any of the other people in whom they may have been living. It is also wise to break any soul ties between the persons who shared the demon.

10. A false Jesus may show up in faith picturing. During inner healing, it is usually helpful to ask the person to picture Jesus in the painful event being remembered. Occasionally, the person will report that "Jesus" looks funny or is doing or saying something that is uncharacteristic, such as hurting or abusing the person. Recently, a man reported that Jesus looked very dark, hairy, and ugly. Another reported that Jesus had a knife in his hand. In both cases, the person in the picture turned out to be an imposter.

How demons can do this, I don't know. And, thankfully, it doesn't happen often. But be on your guard and say something like the following: "If this is not the true Jesus, I command you to disappear." It is wise to say "if," since we may be mistaken. I have been mistaken several times.

After such a challenge, God usually confirms in some way

when the person has indeed seen the true Jesus. Once you have commanded the false Jesus to go and he has disappeared, ask the true Jesus to reveal himself to the person. The person often will see Jesus dressed in shiny clothes and surrounded by light. If the person doesn't see Jesus right away, suggest looking behind. For some reason, Jesus often stands there in faith pictures.

11. Demons may not speak your language. Some seem to be bi- or multilingual. These usually start in another language but when commanded to speak English, will. A missionary in West Africa once told us she challenged a demon in English and it responded in French. When commanded to respond in English, it did. Others, however, won't respond in English, though they understand it.

I don't know whether some demons are monolingual and others bi- or multilingual, or whether they are simply obstinate. I have worked with several Chinese demons that would not speak English, though they understood what I was saying in English. I had to rely on an interpreter to let me know what the demon was saying. This makes things very difficult.

12. Demons are often empowered by vows leading to "soul ties." Quite often people will make an inner vow such as, "I will *never* be like my mother/father" or "I will *never* trust a man again," or even "I *will* be like so-and-so." Often such vows are made as protective measures against hurt. They, however, commit a person for or against some person or thing. They also set up another person as the standard of behavior. This seems to play into some rule in the spiritual sphere that can provide a demon with a place to attach. Perhaps it is the rule against idolatry, since such vows often seem to hinder a person in giving complete allegiance to Jesus.

Unnatural attachment to a person or thing such as that brought about by a vow creates a "soul tie." *A soul tie is a spiritual bonding empowered by Satan between a person and another per-*

son or thing. God has given us the ability to bond. And when that bonding is done in his name, it is a wonderful, enriching and freeing thing. Enslavement results, however, when the Enemy empowers bonding activities such as sexual relationships, blood covenants, giving someone else authority over the self, and dedication to material things such as wealth or occupation. All such bondings need to be broken to bring the freedom God wants.

Frequently, the person has depended heavily on vows and soul ties as insulation against further injury and may be unconscious of their presence and danger. Though we sometimes discover them through things the person says, more frequently they come to light through a word of knowledge or by forcing the demon to tell us they are there. The person needs to renounce the vow(s) and soul ties and to pledge trust in Jesus alone to fill the need the vow once filled.

My associate, Ellen Kearney, shares the following story illustrating the vow problem. Donna, survivor of a traumatic childhood and years of living on the street with her children, had sincerely opened herself up to the Lord. She had been receiving ministry for several months and had been making good progress. At one session, we suggested dealing with Donna's relationship with her mother. She immediately denied there was any problem. Though she seemed deeply angry at her mother, Donna told us with much passion that, no matter what, she would defend and protect her mother against anyone who criticized or attacked her.

Finally, Donna agreed to pray about it, although she expected nothing to come of it. Demons were contacted and the information we gathered led us to ask Donna to give Jesus her feelings of disappointment and anger toward her mother for not protecting and providing for her. She did, and was amazed to find that she felt greatly relieved. But the demons still had a grip. As we prayed, then, a word of knowledge came that she needed to give the Lord charge of her mother. So a team member challenged her to hand over to

Jesus "that little mother you keep in your heart."

At that, the demon yelled, "Hey, how did you know that?" It became obvious Donna was still hanging onto a vow she had made to be her mother's protector. This vow gave the demons power over her. The demons were, however, expelled easily once she renounced the vow and trusted Jesus fully to take care of her mother.

13. Curses can give the Enemy a grip. We have dealt with curses from time to time in the preceding pages, so we will not go into detail here. It should be added, however, that a person in a deliverance ministry must constantly be looking for them. As with vows, the person is usually not aware of curses. We usually need to rely, therefore, on experience, word of knowledge, or information from the demons to discover a curse.

It is common, for example, for people with a low self-image to have unconsciously cursed themselves or some part of them (usually their body or some part of it). When I ask a demon if this person has cursed herself or himself, the answer often is "Yes." To break self-curses, all the person has to do is to renounce them. Anyone who has pronounced a curse can retract it.

If curses have been put on by someone else, a demon usually will readily reveal their presence but will be more reluctant to tell who put them on. Sometimes simply rejecting such curses is sufficient to break them, but often one needs to know who put them on, in order to speak specifically against the curses at their source. When we ask God to reveal who put them on, however, he usually shows us rather quickly. If this information doesn't come, however, speak against the curses anyway.

We are commanded to bless those who curse us (Lk 6:28; Rom 12:14). It is, therefore, important for the person to forgive and bless the curser (including oneself if that is the source). One formula some of us like is, "I return this curse on [name of person] as a blessing from God for the purpose of…"

14. A person may feel worse after a deliverance session. As should be obvious by now, getting people free is a process rather than a one-time event. Just as it takes a person time to develop problems, so it takes time to get them healed. This means that a person has gotten used to living with the problems and has established some kind of equilibrium with the demons and the garbage present. Any change in that equilibrium, then, can feel bad to the ministry recipient.

Deliverance and inner healing require spiritual surgery. As with psychological counseling, this process usually involves new pain, since it requires honesty about things in our lives that are not functioning properly. That honesty is painful in itself. But more pain comes as the malfunctions are cut out, leaving emotional wounds similar to the wounds surgeons leave after operations to heal physical ailments. We all have talked to people who have experienced post-operative pain. They know, however, that it is the pain of healing rather than of continuing illness.

With emotional and spiritual healing, it may not be so obvious to the recipient that after-ministry pain is normal. The person may be looking for a "quick fix." And sometimes God gives inner healing and deliverance without pain. But often what clients face is a lot of reorganizing of their life to learn how to get along without the demons and the emotional and spiritual defense mechanisms depended upon for so long. The removal of demons often uncovers wounds the person has not been aware of. While these now can be dealt with in God's power, the person may undergo discouragement at first.

The one who ministers deliverance needs to be very sensitive to this possibility and to specialize in encouraging people who are troubled by it. The person needs to be reminded of the things God has already done and helped to learn to expect the continuation of such experiences. Supportive persons are needed to lean on and confide in as the healing process continues. God has provided churches to meet this need. If a church group can cooperate with the team as the inner healing continues, that is ideal.

See question 27 in chapter eleven for more on this topic.

BEYOND THE TWISTS AND TURNS

As I have indicated several times throughout this book, there is a lot I don't understand about this ministry. And not understanding is hard for a professor to accept. I am expected to understand things, even mysterious things. And it is truly humbling to have to admit that I don't understand much.

But, to return to the point made at the beginning of this chapter, I am so excited to be constantly involved in doing things that are far beyond my own abilities that what I don't understand doesn't matter a lot to me. As long as God is close and freeing people as he promised he would (Lk 4:18-19), I can rejoice. And I can recommend to you the verses that God has brought me back to over and over again in this ministry: "Trust in the Lord with all your heart. *Never rely on what you think you know.* Remember [= rely on] the Lord in everything you do, and he will show you the right way. Never let yourself think that you are wiser than you are; simply obey the Lord and refuse to do wrong" (Prv 3:5-7).

So, go for it, even without understanding it all! It's worth it.

ELEVEN

Questions and Answers

I've found the question and answer parts of books on deliverance and inner healing very helpful. So, as a way of covering new questions and of summarizing answers already given to others, I will devote this chapter to dealing briefly with questions often asked.

QUESTIONS I CANNOT ANSWER

Lisa had been brought up in a satanist family. Her father and especially her mother had misused her and also given or "rented" her to many others. She had been involved in blood rituals and other horrible activities from her earliest memories and had become infested with hundreds of demons. As we worked with her week by week, rejoicing in the "ups" and struggling with her through the "downs," she asked a series of very disturbing questions.

1. One set of questions centered around the query, "Why did God let all this horrible stuff happen to me?" This was one of Lisa's first questions and one that comes up frequently. If God is who we believe him to be, why would he allow a child to be molested and raped repeatedly? Why would he let her be born into a satanist family at all? Does he love others but not care about Lisa (and the many others in like situations)?

215

I have no idea how to answer such questions, and it hurts. Even as I sit writing, recalling the agony in the voices of countless people asking this question, I ache, the tears come, and I struggle with anger at God for allowing such things to happen. For I'm used to being able to handle whatever questions are put to me. But I have no explanation for this one.

Oh, I can talk about God giving free will to his creatures and the fact that parents and others can use that free will to abuse those they have power over. And I believe this is true. But why he set things up with so little protection for the innocent doesn't make sense to me.

So, when someone asks me this question, I simply say, "I don't know the answer," and go on to assert what I do know. First, *I know that God is good.* I know he loves and cares for people and that he has the power and the desire to help anyone who comes to him for help. Second, *I know that God seldom if ever answers "why" questions.* He didn't answer Job's questions about how he is running the universe and he won't answer ours. So we, like Job, have to be content with how things are, trusting him even if he were to end our life right now (Jb 13:15).

Third, *I do know what Satan wants to do to the one being ministered to* (and to all of us). His job is to kill and destroy (Jn 10:10). So I reason that if the Enemy was not able to destroy this person, a Protector with greater power than Satan must have been there. That protector was Jesus. And, finally, *I know the power of Jesus to free a person from the grip of the Enemy.* Though I can't fully explain why God allows what he allows, I do know he can and will use his power to free people. Those who are willing to work with Jesus toward freedom, even though they cannot understand how, find that he is indeed able to free them.

2. Another series of questions Lisa asked centered around the cry, "Why is it so hard for me?" Why do I have to work so hard to gain freedom while others seem to get off without much of a struggle? Can't God with all his power simply "zap" me into freedom immediately?

Yes, Lisa, he could make you completely free immediately. And I cannot explain why he doesn't. It's just that usually he doesn't bring us freedom unless we work hard with him to bring it about. Does he work this way because he wants us to experience the thrill of participating with him in our move toward health? I don't know.

What I do know, though, is that if we keep working with him, he keeps working with us (Rom 8:28). And the result is more and more of the freedom we crave. The rest I can't explain.

3. Another set of questions asked by many (including me) boil down to, "Why don't demons leave immediately as they did for Jesus?" As I said regarding myth three in chapter two, I wish I knew. It would take a good bit less time and energy. Probably if we could achieve the degree of intimacy Jesus had with the Father it would happen that way. As it is, I am very pleased that God sees fit to involve me at all in his work of banishing demons and bringing freedom to people. So, until I can do it as quickly as Jesus did, I plan to continue to do things the slow way. See that myth for more on this question.

QUESTIONS I CAN AT LEAST TRY TO ANSWER

1. Can cast-out demons return? The answer is, "Yes," unless two conditions have been met: They have been forbidden to return and the garbage has been eradicated. If the emotional and spiritual garbage the demons have been feeding on is still in the person, they have a right to come back, and the person may not be strong enough to keep them away. If, however, they have been forbidden to return, they will have to work from outside the person, since they cannot reenter.

Demons seek bodies and will do all they can to reenter one they have been kicked out of. But they cannot reenter if they have no legal right to be there or if they have been forbidden in the power of Christ to reenter. The newly-freed person, however, can often be fooled into thinking demons are still inside if they speak from outside. The person may then fall into some of the old patterns of attitude and behavior, creating more garbage for those demons (if they haven't been forbidden reentrance) or others (if the original ones can't get in).

As we seek to free people, remember to forbid the demons to return or to send any others. As near as I can tell, none that I have forbidden to return has. On a few occasions, though, I've found that the person has lapsed back into old behavior patterns and allowed others serving the same function(s) back in. For example, after we had cast a spirit of death out of a lady, she attempted suicide again. This allowed another spirit of death in.

Also, counseling is important for the newly-freed person. Though the demons are gone, the person must work with Jesus to overcome old habits. Otherwise, more garbage is created. Determination is required to choose the right thing over the natural inclination to do the habitual. The person also needs to use God-given authority and power to send away any demons that seek entrance.

2. Where should we send demons? Some say we should send them to the abyss or to Satan. I've found that demons tend to react very strongly and negatively to either of these suggestions. Their negative reaction is not very important, except to indicate that they think we have the power to send them to either place. And perhaps we do, though Scripture doesn't seem to confirm it.

I like to play it safe, though, and send them to Jesus. He knows what to do with them. So I usually command them to "Go to the feet of Jesus." Or, if I've commanded them to get into a locked box, I ask angels to carry the box to the feet of Jesus. I command the head demon to tell me when they are at Jesus' feet and then ask Jesus to do what he wants with them. I usually then plant the cross and the empty tomb of

Jesus between the person and the demons and forbid them ever to return or send any others.

3. How do we know when demons are really gone? It is not always easy to determine. Demons often become silent in the final stages of a deliverance, both because they are weak and to give you the impression they have gone. When they do this to me, God often gives me a word of knowledge enabling me to call their bluff. But often the key is simply persistence. On numerous occasions, after I was pretty sure they were gone, I challenged them one more time, and found they were still there.

The first rule is to make sure you've dealt with all the garbage. When you think they should go rather easily but they don't, it may be because something is still in the person's life that needs cleansing. Knowing this, I usually force demons to tell me or the person what remains. When all has been handled, then, I'll often ask, "Are you ready to go now?" Surprisingly, they usually indicate they know it's all over for them.

I find that if I ask God to let the person see when they leave, he usually does. So I often ask for a picture of the angels lowering a box over the demons, locking them into it and taking the locked box to Jesus. While the demons are in the box, I talk to the head demon to make sure what is happening. He tells me if all the demons are in the box, if it has been taken to Jesus, and any other details we need to know.

Sometimes the head demon, though in the box himself, reveals that one or more of the demons under him are still outside. Recently, for example, a head spirit of death was in the box with most of his underlings. When challenged with, "Are all of your demons in the box?" he admitted that the spirit of fear was still outside. I then challenged fear, determined what he was still clinging to and dealt with that. He then got into the box and the angels carried the box to Jesus.

Once the box of demons is at Jesus' feet, I ask him to dispose of it and let the person see what he does with it. The person will usually see him crush it, throw it away, cast it into a pit, or simply make it disappear. When it is truly gone, I will not be able to get any reply from the demons and the person will usually feel a distinct release. I then plant the cross and the tomb between the person and the demons and say something like, "I seal in Jesus' name whatever he has done here."

4. If a person renounces a demon, does it automatically leave? Sometimes mere renunciation is sufficient to get a demon out. This has enabled some persons to cast demons out of themselves. Most often, however, even after the inner healing work has been done, a person's renunciation of a demon needs to be followed by the authoritative command for it to leave. Sometimes it is sufficient for this command to come from the demonized person. More often, however, it needs to come from someone else.

5. Should a person attempt self-deliverance? Yes. Part of our journey into the power aspect of Christianity is learning who we are in Christ. As children of the King, we inherit the right to rule and to wield our Father's power both on behalf of others and on behalf of ourselves. Learning to rebuke the Enemy and to thwart his schemes in our own lives sets us well on the way to gaining and keeping our freedom from demonic invasion.

But not everyone seems to be able to do self-deliverance. To try it, challenge the spirit(s) inside in the same way you would challenge one in another. Force it to tell you what it is attached to and deal with each issue as it comes to mind. When the demon can bring up no new issues, cast it out by sending it to the feet of Jesus in the way suggested above.

6. How do I know whether to believe a demon? Never believe a demon without testing as much of the information as possible. Often the person will know whether what is being said is the truth or not. Confirmation also may be made by using the information for dealing with inner issues, discovering those were indeed important, and that dealing with them has weakened the demon(s).

As pointed out in chapter eight where we dealt more fully with this subject, demons will try to bluff and deceive even when commanded to speak the truth in Jesus' name. Get whatever information you can from them, but use it cautiously and depend on the Holy Spirit and the demonized person to confirm it. God will often give words of knowledge to confirm or refute what demons say.

7. What if we don't get all the demons out in one session? Under at least two conditions we won't get the job finished. There may be just too much to do in one session, so work at getting rid of the rats session by session until they are completely gone. The other situation is when you think they are gone but they aren't.

The keys are patience and not getting discouraged. The conditions under which the demonization happened are usually complex. It is no wonder, then, if it takes awhile to get everything cleaned up. So do what you and the Holy Spirit feel is the right amount in any given session, forbid the remaining demons to do their jobs between sessions, and make another appointment. Assign the person, meanwhile, to do those things that will weaken the demons, such as praising, worshiping, Bible reading, praying, and dealing with emotional and spiritual problems.

8. Can a person with demons inside minister deliverance to others? The answer is definitely, "Yes." I have seen it happen many times, though always with people who were either in the process of getting freed themselves or ignorant of the fact that they too were demonized. These were people who either had no idea they were infested or knew but were nonetheless working regularly toward their own release. I would not recommend ministering in deliverance for demonized persons who are not willing to work on getting themselves free. There would be too much likelihood that their demons would interfere.

When someone on a team is demonized but doesn't know it, interesting things can happen. Often that person's demons respond to commands given to the demons in the person being helped. Or, they may try to help the demons under attack by causing a scene, disrupting the session by diverting attention. Or they may simply interfere in some way with their host, alerting that person to their presence. This happened once while my team was dealing with a spirit of incubus (a spirit who attacks women sexually). A female team member felt definite interference as we gained control and expelled Incubus from the other woman. Afterwards, we took additional time to get our teammate free from a demon of this same name and function that lived in her.

When I know that a team member still has demons inside, I claim special protection for all of us from them and forbid them to assist their colleagues in any way. I say these things, however, in a general way so as to not embarrass the member(s) in question. I say something like, "I speak protection to us all from any representatives of the Enemy resident in any of us and forbid any of them to interfere in any way in the ministry at hand."

If you are aware that you still have demons inside you, don't shy away from ministering to others. Do, however, claim protection for yourself and the others in a way similar to the above. You may do this silently, so others in the group are not aware of your problem.

9. Can I become demonized by touching a demonized person? I have found some people obsessed with fear that they can contract demons by touching a demonized person. Some even believe that those doing deliverance should refrain from touching the person lest they become infested themselves.

As usual, the truth is more complicated. There are rules. One is that if you are vulnerable, you can get demons from someone else. Another is that demons are not limited to "jumping on" those who touch the person they inhabit. They can go through the air just as easily as they can follow the arm of a person who lays hands on their host. A third rule is that if people are protected by the power of the Holy Spirit, demonic spirits cannot get at them.

So, claim God's protection constantly, not just when ministering. We are surrounded by demonized people. And in ministry, don't be afraid to touch the person you are ministering to. Often they need to be touched lovingly. It's important, though, to ask their permission for any touching. If they have been abused, you may have to win their confidence before any touching would be appropriate. Better not to touch than to do something that might be misperceived.

10. Should couples receive ministry together? It is often good to minister to couples together since shared demons, not to mention shared information and insight, are likely. Married couples are united in their spirits. Beyond the fact that they may share demonization problems, it is important that they gain freedom together. Furthermore, it is important to develop a supportive attitude between the two concerning the changes taking place. If one is ministered to individually, it is good to minister to the other as soon as possible.

One or the other partner may, however, want to work alone on some problem. If it is something being kept secret, there should be prayer and discussion concerning if and how to share it with the other partner. Though there may be times when a secret should continue to be kept secret, the ideal would be for everything to be shared between the husband the wife. If, however, the relationship is poor or the openness of the partner in doubt, this may not be the time. In any event, sharing with the partner after the problem is solved may be wiser than while the one being ministered to is still struggling with it.

On occasion, one partner is unreceptive to ministry for either member. Still, it is better to work with the receptive one than with neither. I have had several occasions when the other partner was so impressed with the changes in the one who came for help that he or she then asked for help. One such partner came to say, "My husband is so different, I'd like to receive the same kind of ministry. Perhaps I can change too!"

11. Can I minister to an unwilling person? As I've already indicated, it is very difficult to minister to someone who is unwilling. There are people close to me who badly need inner healing and probably deliverance, but they will not let it happen. This hurts—perhaps as much as it hurt Jesus to see the rich young man turn away (Mk 10:17-22). Mark says, Jesus loved that man (v. 21), but he had to respect the man's decision. Jesus neither reduced his requirements nor went chasing after him.

I believe that Jesus' often-repeated statement, "Your faith has made you whole" (Mt 9:22; Mk 5:34; 10:52; Lk 8:48; 17:19) is basically a statement concerning the person's choice to pursue wholeness and to pursue it in the right place. Without that willingness, even determination, not even God would act to heal the person. My policy, then, is not to work with anyone who is knowingly unwilling, unless it be to help the person to become willing.

Many times, however, we find a person who has sought ministry is *unconsciously unwilling*. Especially if the ministry is already underway, I see it as my task to help the person become both willing and determined to work with God and us to solve the problem. Often, therefore, I try to bring about one or more small demonstrations of God's power and good will toward the person to bring a boost to the person's faith and confidence in God. Among the "little" things I use are the healing of a headache, or the receiving of a hug from Jesus, or the flow of peace that comes from being blessed with peace.

12. What should we do if a person's will is being strongly interfered with by a demon? I have said that demons can live in a Christian's mind, emotions, and will. I have also pointed out that the person's will needs to be strongly engaged in the process if demons are to be cast out. For this reason, if I perceive demonic activity to be strong in the person's will, I attempt to take the person's will from the demon early in the game.

To do this, I say to the demon something like, "In the name of Jesus, we claim so-and-so's will. We cancel your authority and break your power over it. If [name of person] has given it to you, we renounce and reject that permission and take [name of person] will for Jesus."

Often, thus taking the person's will gives immediate strength for the process. Often, however, the demon will battle for the person's will since he knows that if he loses that, he's in big trouble. Usually claiming the will as suggested above will result in at least partial release. If it does not, you need to go back to do whatever inner healing the person (and the demon) permit while coming back again and again, in the attempt to take the person's will fully for Christ.

13. Can I minister to my family or friends? Ministering to family members and friends can be difficult but also very meaningful. The person receiving ministry needs to be comfortable with the one ministering if anything worthwhile is to result. Often a person with an intimate relationship with a team member feels threatened.

Each case has to be evaluated independently. Everything depends on the kind of relationship involved and the openness of the person receiving ministry. Never try to force someone close to you, no matter how much you feel that person could benefit from your ministry. Even if someone close to you is open, it is usually best to find someone else whom you both trust. Leave it up to your loved one, then, whether you are to be involved. Help the person to feel completely free to reject your participation and hold no hard feelings. The important thing is to get that person free, not for you to be involved.

14. If I get into a deliverance ministry, is my family in danger? Unfortunately, the answer is "Yes." The Enemy doesn't like it when people fight against him, so he will attack whoever may be vulnerable in attempting to get us to stop attacking him. If we have family members who are vulnerable because of undealt-with garbage in their lives, they are likely to be attacked.

There are at least two lines of defense. The first, of course, is to get our family members to deal with their problems and become invulnerable. Second, they can be protected to some extent by our prayers (especially praying by the head of the family). We can and should regularly take authority over family members and forbid the Enemy to attack them. This seems to inhibit external attacks, but not to deter demons when invitations are extended by the persons themselves.

A difficult choice has to be made. Many who move into a deliverance ministry find they have family members who will not work at getting free from their own captivity. The Enemy, therefore, takes revenge on the family member(s) whenever he wants to put pressure on the person who is bothering him. One has to choose, then, between working in deliverance at the risk of Enemy attacks on loved ones and dropping the idea and thereby playing into the Enemy's hands. I strongly recommend against the latter, no matter what the cost.

15. What should we do when a demon threatens us? In a recent bout with a demon, I heard for the umpteenth time the threat, "I'll kill you!" But, since I had already prayed protection over the team and all persons and things associated with us, I simply said to him, "You can't do it. I'm protected." And he knew he couldn't hurt me.

As mentioned several times, demons are largely bluff. If they can get you off their backs through such threats, they will. This knowledge combined with the power of God to protect is our major weapon. If, when threatened, I realize I have forgotten to speak protection over us, I simply speak it after the threat and it is just as effective. I say something like, "I claim the power of the Holy Spirit to protect me, all others here and all who are in any way associated with us from such a threat." You can in this way cancel any threat demons make.

16. Can demons get help from other demons while we are ministering? The answer is "Yes," unless you cut them off from such help. I first learned this while working with a young man with a spirit of homosexuality. As I challenged the demon, I noticed that the young man's eyes were raised and he seemed to be searching the sky for something. I perceived that the demon was calling for help, and forbade it. That seemed to change the strength of the demon noticeably.

What I do routinely now is to include in the opening prayer the forbidding of any such help. I will say something like, "I cut off any demons inside this person from receiving any help either from outside or from inside." In addition to the forbidding of help from outside, I also forbid the banding together of the demons inside to strengthen the one we're working on.

17. What if the demon seems too strong to get out? Often, especially in your early attempts to work in deliverance, you will find that demons seem too strong. There could be several reasons for this. For one, the demon may simply be bluffing. He may not be powerful but may think he can fool you into thinking he has a stronger grip than he really has. Or, he may be getting help from other demons, outside or inside. You can prevent this by cutting off any help from demons outside or inside.

Or, the work of inner healing may not have gone far enough to weaken the demons to the point where it is easy to get them out. There may still be stuff that they have a grip on. If so, go back and do more inner healing. If you can't get information about what additional inner healing needs to be done from the demon in charge, call up one of the weaker ones. Often they will give you the information you need more easily. Also, be careful to assure that the person is fully cooperating in the process, all the while praying silently that God will reveal what needs to be done. Once, when I was at such an impasse with a young man, he suddenly confessed a major sin that he'd been hiding. This broke the demon's grip and he was soon gone.

If all seems to fail, bring the session to a close. It is often good to take such a break to allow the Holy Spirit to bring to mind things that didn't come up during the first session. At such a time I will often confine the demons to a box until approached again in Jesus' name, forbid them to hear the plans we make, and work out a strategy. It is good to assign the person to do some spiritual homework—praying, worship, Bible reading—and to spend some time reflecting under the guidance of the Holy Spirit on what may yet need to be dealt with. Often, the person will have dealt with at least some of the remaining problems before the next session, and the demons will be significantly weaker.

18. Is ministry to those involved in satanism and the occult harder? The answer usually is "Yes." Occult demons are believed by some to have greater power than ordinary demons. In any event, the fact that a person has willingly chosen involvement with occult demons, or that an adult in authority over a child has dedicated that child to demonic beings, seems to give their demons a stronger grip than that of demons resulting from emotional hurt or even sin.

In addition, those who have been involved in the occult, either willingly or as victims of satanic ritual abuse, are often subject to strong efforts by the people involved to keep them from defecting. Anne was such a person. She was a practicing witch who had come to a seminar with the intent of causing disturbances. While there, Anne was led to the Lord and confessed that she had been seeking a way out of her bondage to the coven and her evil lifestyle.

Later, Anne was aided in cleansing her home of occult objects and demonic intruders. She immediately began to suffer severe demonic attacks through illness and accidents. It was learned that other witches were behind these attacks. Anne also received many threats from her former associates. She has kept her faith, though it has had many ups and downs.

In ministering to such people, it is essential to be as invulnerable as possible. Our own garbage needs to be dealt with. We need to pray ourselves and to have others praying both for us and our families, especially any who may be more vulnerable to demonic attacks (for example, children and non-Christian relatives). We need also to speak against curses coming our way. These may be directed at our person, others involved in the ministry, property, relationships, jobs, finances, or anything else pertaining to us. Though there is risk, don't let the Enemy keep you from ministering to these needy people because of fear. Fear does not come from God (2 Tm 1:7).

19. What role do demons play in physical problems? Demons will do whatever they can to trouble and harass a person, especially those who can cause them difficulty, such as Christians. They can, however, only work with weaknesses that are already there. If, for example, they want to assist germs in causing a cold, they'll not be able to if the person's resistance (both physical and spiritual) is too great. I ministered to a thirty-five-year-old man I'll call Loren who had a spirit of failure. This man had become very serious about his commitment to Christ early in his teenage years. He was also very good at basketball and other sports. When Loren was fourteen, Failure found a weakness in one of Loren's hips and disabled him. When asked if he was the one who had caused the hip problem, Failure replied, "Of course. He was getting too good [at basketball]. I had to make him fail!"

I had an interesting confirmation that demons need weakness to do their work while working with a woman who had suffered frequent epileptic fits until she had surgery to prevent them. I asked the demon if he was the one behind the fits. He said, "Yes." Why then, I asked, wasn't the woman hav ing the fits anymore? He replied, "Because of the operation." Apparently, the demon could bring them about only as long as she had a physical weakness. When that weakness was repaired, the demon could no longer cause the attacks.

In the case of accidents, demons can take advantage of natural weaknesses to bring them about. Then they can take advantage of damage from the accident to make things worse. When the person has a systemic weakness related to emotional or physical problems and then has an accident, demons like to get involved to slow down the healing process.

I found this tactic had played a strong role in the problem of a woman who came to one of our seminars. I'll call her Emily. Emily had fallen and hurt her right side while playing volleyball. Though the doctor treated Emily competently, after two weeks he was surprised to note that her condition, far from improving, had deteriorated seriously.

In ministering to Emily, we discovered a lot of inner garbage stemming from her upbringing. We also found demons attached to the garbage. Because Emily had weaknesses derived from nursing anger, bitterness, and low self-esteem, the demons were able to inhibit her body's defense system. Healing of the physical problems brought on by her accident, then, had to start with inner healing and getting rid of the demons. Once we had made a good start on the garbage and expelled several demons, Emily no longer needed the crutches on which she had come to the seminar.

Demons can also attach to disabilities and propensities toward disease that have been inherited. In many cases, the demon has also been inherited with the disability or tendency. In other cases, the physical tendency has been inherited and a demon has been able to attach to it after conception. In either case, both the physical problem and the demon(s) have to be dealt with. It is usually best to get rid of the demon(s) before praying over the physical problem. Whatever course is taken, remember to see the person as a whole. Don't simply focus on a single aspect (physical, emotional, or spiritual) of the overall problem.

20. Is a compulsion toward suicide always demonic? Though it is quite typical of demons, especially spirits of death, to push their hosts toward suicide, we cannot conclude that such an urge is always demonic. If, however, I find a person with strong suicidal tendencies, I always look for a spirit of death or a spirit of suicide. They are usually there.

21. Is it helpful to use gestures, anointing oil, or other such techniques? A rule of thumb might be, *Whatever bothers the demon(s) is a good thing to use,* if it doesn't bother the person too much. I have found the following effective with some demons but not with others: anointing oil (empowered by God through blessing it), eye contact, touching the person, inviting angels to torment the demons, making the sign of the cross, speaking in tongues, having the person drink water that has been blessed, forcing the demons first to see Jesus and then to face and look at him, speaking light into dark places where demons live, and threatening to send them to Satan or into the abyss. In addition, some deliverance ministers find it helpful to baptize the person, serve the Lord's Supper to the person, and use blessed salt giving a few grains to the person every hour. I have found no method that consistently works well. The closest is forcing demons to look into Jesus' face. They do not like that.

We need to be careful not to reduce deliverance to a set of techniques. However, the Holy Spirit often uses such things as these quite effectively.

22. What should be done with cursed or dedicated objects? Most religious groups, including Christians, dedicate certain material objects to their god(s). Most Christian groups dedicate at least their church buildings and certain objects used in worship. We should do more of this, for dedicated objects are empowered by God.

Within cults and non-Christian religions, dedications to Satan and his representatives are very common. In addition, these groups seek to do harm by placing curses on material objects that are then given to others. Objects dedicated to the satanic kingdom are very dangerous for Christians to own. Yet many have bought such objects unwittingly (often overseas) and keep them in their homes. Others have received gifts that carry satanic powers from relatives or friends in occult groups.

A colleague of mine, C. Peter Wagner, was puzzled by strange things happening in his home. Friends with gifts of discernment discovered that the source was artifacts brought home from Bolivia, where he had been a missionary. A man to whom I ministered in Cyprus found two rings and a necklace given him by close relatives to be infested.

As a rule, occult paraphernalia should be destroyed, since its only purpose is to carry satanic power. Other things, such as jewelry, can, however, be stripped of satanic power and invested with God's power. Dedications or curses can be broken over objects in the same way they can be broken over people. In Jesus' name, take authority over anything suspicious and cancel all satanic empowerment that may be in it. Then forbid the return of demons attached to the object. It is my custom, then, to bless the object in the name of Jesus with his power to bring blessing to whoever uses it. This is what we did with the jewelry mentioned above. Wagner, however, chose to destroy the objects in his home. A friend who had been a life-long Freemason, once he had accepted Christ and learned of the evils of Freemasonry, chose to destroy all the artifacts he had accumulated from that cult. Though his conversion was undoubtedly the major factor in the drastic change in his life, perhaps some of his newfound freedom came as a result of the repudiation of his thirty-four year attachment to that group and the destruction of all symbols of that loyalty.

When artifacts are kept, one should keep a high level of consciousness of what they once were, lest the demons return to them. It is likely that demons will try to retake material objects as they do with people after they have been banished from them. If, however, they have been forbidden to return, I doubt that they can come back.

23. Is special preparation for a deliverance session necessary? As already indicated, I always try to be ready for ministry to the demonized. So I seldom prepare specially by fasting or longer times of prayer and Bible study. Some of my colleagues, however, always make special preparations. Perhaps because of this, some of them have ministry gifts I don't have. The fact that I have quite a number of people regularly interceding for me is, I believe, an important factor in the gifts I do have.

I do, however, fast and pray before a session I expect to be more difficult. If the person has been in the occult, for example, or if we have had a less than successful previous session, I will prepare specially.

24. Can demons be cast out over the telephone? Yes, I've done it several times. Though working face to face is preferable, I've had people in need of deliverance call me on the phone from some distance away. I've gone ahead and had good success.

The key is to make contact with the demon(s) and gain control over them. Sometimes this is more difficult or, at least, takes longer over the phone than in person. In a couple of instances, I've had to abandon the attempt. I've found it easier to establish telephone contact and control when I've previously worked with the person. In one of my first tries over the phone, the demon was put out when he wasn't able to escape. Though when contact was first established, he was arrogant, bragging, "You'll not get me," later he changed his tune. "This is disgusting!" was his comment.

The Holy Spirit is capable of dealing with demons whether over the phone or in person. Ministering by phone, however, makes it impossible to "track" visibly what's going on. It's also difficult to regain contact with the person or the demon if the demon succeeds in keeping the person from speaking or causes the phone to be dropped. Though ministering over the phone is not ideal, it is worth the try.

25. Can animals be demonized? Yes. Jesus sent the demons called Legion into a herd of pigs (Lk 8:26-38). I once ministered to a four-year-old boy whom demons caused to run into walls. He had a cat that did the same thing. We had to cast demons out of both. I've heard of a woman who suspected her baby parakeet to have a demon and tested the theory by commanding it to perform a trick it had never been taught. It complied immediately and a demon was later cast out of it.

Demons can inhabit animals and through them exert influence over humans. Animals can be demonized purposely by those who wish to use them in witchcraft and the like, or they may acquire demons through contact with demonized people, most often their owners. The danger exists of satanists demonizing and selling or giving pets to people they seek to infect.

If you suspect demonization in an animal, treat it as you would a material object that has been dedicated or cursed (see question 22 above). Take authority over the demon(s), break their power and command them to leave. When you are sure they've left, bless the animal with the power of Jesus. If this doesn't seem to work, get rid of the animal.

26. How does it feel when a demon speaks through you? As pointed out in chapter two, demons do not fully control the people in whom they reside. But people often fear that letting demons speak through them will give the demons more power over them than they already have. This fear is not valid when we are working under the power of the Holy Spirit, for he controls the process. Because this is so, the person can control if and when the demon can speak.

I once was asked to work with a woman who was devastated when demons inside her began to reply to my challenges. Her reaction was to prevent them from communicating with me. I could not help her, since she sided with them rather than with Jesus. On many other occasions, the one being counseled has said something like, "You wouldn't want to hear what they're saying." That is, the demons were using impolite language directed toward me, so the person withheld from me what they were saying.

When demons inside people respond, they often will hear the answer either vocalized or as an impression from inside their heads. Which occurs depends on two factors: the strength of the demon and how readily the person allows it to speak. Some people, like the woman just mentioned above, are so distraught by the presence of another being inside them that they repress the ability of even quite strong demons to speak. Once they recognize another being is indeed present but that we have authority and power over it, however, they usually cooperate well with the process. Weak demons may not have enough strength to make use of the person's vocal cords. They, therefore, communicate by giving the person impressions that the person then reports to the team.

When demons begin to respond, it is common for people to be confused as to which words are theirs and which are those of the demons. I ask the person to report to me whatever thoughts and impressions come and let me help sort them out. Together, we usually find it easy to make the distinction. In this way we can carry on quite satisfactory conversations with the demons whether they are talking directly through the person's vocal apparatus or communicating by impressions that the person voices.

When such conversations are going on, people feel like an observer of an interaction taking place through their mouth without going through their mind. Usually the first knowledge people have of what comes out of their mouth is when they hear it with their ears.

27. Is improvement immediate when demons are cast out?
When demons are cast out, only part of the healing process has been accomplished. As I have emphasized, dealing with the whole person, especially the emotional and spiritual garbage, is the most important part of the quest for whole-

ness. It is likely, therefore, that gaining freedom from one or more demons will result in one or more troublesome conditions for the person.

Usually people have had to adjust to new feelings, and the adjustment is not always smooth. Sometimes an important part of demonic activity is to suppress emotion. In such cases, release from the demons often means the person will feel pain as well as peace and joy. Such feelings will be unfamiliar to the person and may hurt, giving the impression that now more is wrong rather than less. Such reactions need to be interpreted for the delivered person.

Jennifer (mentioned in chapter three) had been experiencing voices in her head for as long as she could remember and was very happy to have those voices gone after one of our sessions. The self-criticism and ridicule she had been experiencing through those demonic voices were gone. However, Jennifer soon found that she also had depended on those voices for a certain amount of decision-making, and that help was also gone. This meant she had to learn new ways of coming to some kinds of decisions. She became uncomfortable to the point of sometimes wishing the "helpful" demonic voices were back.

Also uncomfortable and sometimes agonizing is the reality that release from demons may uncover more garbage to be dealt with. God's way is the way of truth. Satan's is the way of deceit. Demons regularly deceive people into hiding and refusing to face difficult truths concerning themselves and those who have hurt them. When working with God toward healing uncovers disagreeable truth, problems frequently arise. For example, the person may be able to face truth well enough to get rid of the demon(s) during the ministry session. Afterwards, however, these newly-revealed truths may come crashing in on the person (helped by demons, working now from outside), and cause great pain.

We who work in deliverance and inner healing need to be there for the person during the struggle with such adjustments. Getting through this period is often more difficult than getting through the ministry session(s). One lady reported, "I'm going through an identity crisis. I'm not sure who I am anymore." She had been living with lies for so long, it was both confusing and painful to recognize and accept the horrible truths of her past. The lies she had been believing had, of course, misled her, but they also had protected her from having to face those truths. Living without that cushion was hard for her.

Demons have usually functioned to destroy parts of a person's life and relationships. For example, the person may be immature due to demonic repression of that person's development. With the garbage and the demons gone, the person is faced with the problem of developing the maturity he or she was previously denied.

Relationships with people, often close relatives, often have to be redefined. A woman I'll call Sally was called in by her supervisor a few weeks after God had released her from several demons. He asked two questions: "What's happened to you?" and "Will it last?" Sally now has the problem of redefining her relationships with her work associates, her husband, and just about everybody else in her life. It's not easy.

See Twists and Turns #14 in chapter ten for more on this topic.

28. In multiple personalities, does freeing the core person free others too? The answer is, "Usually no." Ordinarily, demons need to be cast out of each personality separately. Each personality needs to be assessed separately, both for demons and inner healing needs. Not all of the personalities inhabiting the same body may be demonized. Demons will, however, be very anxious to maintain as much disruption as possible. They are active in keeping the personalities separated. They also will often interfere in the deliverance process by causing switching between personalities, unless forbidden.

While it is difficult to understand, those who work with multiples find that each personality has a separate will, separate thoughts, emotions, and spiritual experience. One alter may be a committed Christian, for example, while another may vehemently deny any relationship with Christ. The very nature of the disorder is that each alter has garbage to deal with, so each must be inner-healed and freed of demons individually. Each also needs to be led to Jesus separately. This is the first thing I work toward.

When dealing with the head demon in one alter, we sometimes find that it has control over some demons in other alters, so I order all demons under its control to be bound to it and leave with it. In Teresa's case (see chapter three), a spirit called Guardian was cast out of her core personality and commanded to take all spirits under his control with him. He apparently took demons from several of the personalities. Later, however, one of the personalities (not the core person) called out for and received another guardian spirit that had to be dealt with separately within that personality alone.

ARE THESE ALL THE QUESTIONS THAT NEED ANSWERING?

No, of course not. It is my hope and prayer, though, that these answers, plus the book as a whole, will suffice to take you into a deliverance ministry, where you will be able to discover new answers to these and other questions. You will also, of course, discover new questions—and, hopefully, answers to those questions as well. May God bless you in your quest.

Afterword

AT THE END OF THE SEMINARS I teach on inner healing and deliverance, there is one question that comes up over and over again, "What now?" People wonder what steps to take now that they have listened, observed, and hopefully opened themselves up to new insights and practices in dealing with demons.

It was in answer to just this sort of question at the end of Jesus' ministry that the Master returned to his disciples, blessed them with peace, breathed on them to receive the Holy Spirit, and said, "As the Father sent me, so I send you" (Jn 20:19-22).

These words at the end of our Lord's ministry challenge us to ask why he came. What was the mission God the Father sent Jesus to accomplish and that the Master says we are to continue? He answered this question early in his ministry, while reading the Scriptures in the synagogue of his hometown of Nazareth. He said, "The Spirit of the Lord is upon me, because he has chosen me to bring good news to the poor. He has sent me to proclaim liberty to the captives and recovery of sight to the blind, to set free the oppressed and announce that the time has come when the Lord will save his people" (Lk 4:18-19). He came to the victims (the poor), the captives, the blind, and the oppressed to bring the good news of liberty, recovery, freedom, and rescue.

And at the end of his time on earth, Jesus commissioned

us to follow his example. I ask you to *heed Jesus' commission and to do what he did.* His commissioning of us could not have been clearer. We could not have a better leader and model. We could not have more power and authority available to us. And we have at least a start toward understanding what needs to be done and how to do it. *The question is whether or not we will obey him.*

I have sought to present both spiritual insights and practical tips that will enable you to obey our Lord by doing what he did. I have aimed to decrease ignorance and fear about the ministry of deliverance and to "demystify" the whole subject of demonization. I pray that this book has provided you with enough issues and advice on how to deal with them so that you can begin to minister yourself.

Though I certainly cannot claim infallibility in the perspectives and approaches I've presented, I can guarantee that if you follow these guidelines, you will be a considerable threat to Satan and his kingdom. He does not like it at all when people begin to experiment with such insights. He gets especially angry when we try them and discover that they work. He will, therefore, attempt to keep you from moving forward in this area and will seek to get you to neglect or even reject such ministry

Satan would be delighted if you turned your back on the growing number of testimonies that indicate dark angels are increasingly active and increasingly out in the open, even here in America. He would especially like you to ignore the overwhelming evidence that Christians can be demonized. The Enemy's strategy is clear: if you believe he is no longer active and that he cannot hurt Christians, you will be no threat to him.

Satan would also be happy if you accept the myth that delivering people from demons is a mystical kind of activity that only superspiritual, highly gifted people dare enter. He will do anything possible to keep you from recognizing and using the power and authority Jesus has given us.

So, what will be your perspective?

Even if your perspective puts you right where Jesus wants you, *the Enemy will do whatever he can to keep you from practicing what you know.* As I have heard from many demons, they just want us to leave them alone. "Why have you come?," one said to me. "I told her husband not to invite you. I was just about to finish her off!"

For many of you, this area raises problems of belief. You just cannot believe much of what I'm saying could possibly be true. But for many, it is not belief that hinders you, it is reluctance to act on that belief.

This book is intended to be a call to action. Many of our brothers and sisters are demonized and yearn to be delivered, even if they don't understand the exact nature of their problem. But the Enemy keeps them ignorant of the possibility of freedom, or deceives them into believing that their problem is something else, or tries to make them fearful of what deliverance would involve. This torment will continue unless someone comes along who understands their problem and is bold enough to bring them God's deliverance and healing. God wants you to be that person if you are a believer, God wants you to exercise the authority of Jesus to set the captives free. Here are your marching orders:

1. Recognize that we are at war. There is a kingdom full of dark angels roaming around like lions looking for opportunities to devour whoever they can (1 Pt 5:8). We live in Enemy territory and will be defeated if we do not defend ourselves. We will also lose sisters and brothers if we do not attack the Enemy to free them.

2. Pray. Ask God for boldness. Ask God for others to work with you. Ask God for opportunities. When you have found others, pray with them that God will grant you the right amount of authority, power, insight, and perseverance necessary to do the job. Then, with them, attack the Enemy and defeat him.

3. Recognize that the main difference between you and those of us who regularly minister deliverance is experience, not gifting. We all have the authority of Jesus as believers. We are all gifted in a variety of ways. And most, if not all, of us have some gifts that can be used in a deliverance ministry. You have the same Holy Spirit we have. That means you carry with you at all times infinitely greater power than the whole satanic kingdom put together. Claim that power for protection. Work in that power to attack dark angels and break demonic oppression.

4. Know that you will make mistakes. I wish this wasn't so, but it is. The only way to learn, however, is to launch out in faith, feeling inadequate, risking mistakes, but knowing that God will meet you as you are faithful to him.

5. Don't let your doubts and unresolved questions keep you from stepping out. We all have them. I can't count the number of times I've come away from deliverance sessions asking, "Did that really happen?" Though I ask such questions less now than at the beginning, I still have many questions.

6. Be assured that on our side is a powerful and empowering Lord who is willing to use anyone. On the other side, then, is a kingdom of dark angels working mostly by deceit, fear, and bluff. Jesus has already won the victory. Our job is the rescuing and freeing of the prisoners of war.

7. Don't expect deliverance to always be easy. Sometimes it is. Often it isn't. The Enemy, though he can't possibly win the war, can still win a few battles. You will not always be successful. You will often be painfully aware that you don't fully understand what's going on.

8. What we can understand is that the combination of God's power and the person's will, plus our prayer and perseverance, brings spiritual freedom. When the afflicted person is willing to fight dark angels by dealing with whatever they have a grip on and the ones minis-

tering are persistent in working with God for however long it takes, victory is assured.

9. As you minster, then, expect God to become very real and increasingly close both to those you counsel and to you. As I've said before, it is incredibly growth-producing to be constantly involved in doing things we know we cannot do on our own. You will find your spiritual life growing greatly as you participate with the Master.

So, "do the stuff." Release prisoners. Free captives. Let people know and experience the fact that Jesus is King of Kings and Lord of Lords right now as well as in the future.

I bless each of you with boldness, effectiveness, wisdom, and increasing closeness to Jesus as you carry out his commission to do what he does (Jn 14:12) in defeating dark angels.

Notes

ONE
Are Satan and Dark Angels for Real?

1. Ed Murphy, *Equipping the Saints* (Vol. 4, No. 1, Winter 1990), 27, 29.
2. Ken Blue, *Authority to Heal* (Downers Grove, IL: InterVarsity, 1987), 89.
3. Blue, *Authority to Heal*, 16, 17.

TWO
Twelve Myths Concerning Demonization

1. Merrill Unger, *Demons in the World Today* (Wheaton, IL: Tyndale, 1971), 101.
2. Blue, *Authority to Heal*, 17.
3. James Friesen, *Uncovering the Mystery of MPD* (San Bernardino, CA: Here's Life, 1991), 91.
4. Friesen, *Uncovering the Mystery of MPD*, 101.
5. Charles H. Kraft, *Christianity with Power* (Ann Arbor, MI: Servant, 1989), 134.
6. See chapter eight for a discussion of the ins and outs, ups and downs of getting information from demons.

THREE
Demonization in Christians?

1. Fred C. Dickason, *Demon Possession and the Christian* (Chicago, IL: Moody Press, 1987), 175.
2. Unger, *Demons in the World Today*, 117.
3. Dickason, *Demon Possession and the Christian*, 73-148.
4. Dickason, *Demon Possession and the Christian*, 175-76.
5. Unger, *What Demons Can Do to Saints* (Chicago, IL: Moody Press, 1977), 51, 52.

FOUR
Our Power and Authority

1. Bernard Kelly, *The Seven Gifts* (London: Sheed and Ward, 1941), 12-14.

2. There is a serious issue here that stems from a belief that God's omnipotence means that he can do anything he chooses to do at any time he chooses—even to the extent that he can break the rules by which he runs the universe. In fact, God has given a measure of freedom both to humans and to Satan and his colleagues. When that freedom is used, then, to hurt, God protects his own (as he did with Job), but doesn't prevent things from happening.

We, however, often ignore the significant fact that God did intervene to protect us and interpret the fact that he didn't prevent the hurt as an indication that he is not on our side. On the basis of this misunderstanding, then, we get angry at him and hold bitterness in our hearts against him. These attitudes constitute a challenge to God's authority since they are based on the feeling that we know better than God how the universe should be run. We need, therefore, to repent of such an attitude (as Job had to) and to release God (and ourselves) from our anger. In a certain sense, this might be described as "forgiving" God.

SIX
Demonic Attachment and Strength

1. From a prepublication chapter entitled "The New Age: Satan's Subtle Deception" by Elizabeth Mahoney.
2. Kraft, *Christianity with Power*, 129-30.

SEVEN
Dealing with the Garbage through Inner Healing

1. Betty Tapscott, *Inner Healing through Healing of Memories* (Kingwood, TX: Hunter Publishing, 1975), 13.
2. David Seamands, *Healing of Memories* (Wheaton, IL: Victor, 1985), 24.
3. Seamands, *Healing of Memories*, 24.

Bibliography

American Psychiatric Association. *The Diagnostic and Statistical Manual of Mental Disorders* (third edition), 1980.

Anderson, Neil. *Victory over the Darkness* (Ventura, CA: Regal, 1990). *The Bondage Breaker* (Eugene, OR: Harvest House, 1990).

Arnold, Clinton E. *Ephesians: Power and Magic* (Cambridge: Cambridge Univ., 1989).

Basham, Don. *Can a Christian Have a Demon?* (Monroeville, PA: Whitaker House, 1971). *Deliver Us from Evil* (Old Tappan, NJ: Revell, 1972, 1980).

Bernal, Dick. *Curses* (Shippensburg, PA: Companion Press, 1991).

Birch, George A. *The Deliverance Ministry* (Cathedral City, CA: Horizon, 1988).

Blue, Ken. *Authority to Heal* (Downers Grove, IL: InterVarsity, 1987).

Bubeck, Mark. *The Adversary* (Chicago, IL: Moody Press, 1975). *Overcoming the Adversary* (Chicago, IL: Moody Press, 1984). *The Satanic Revival* (San Bernardino, CA: Here's Life, 1991).

Cabezas, Rita. *Des Enmascarado* (Published privately in Costa Rica). Reference here taken from unpublished English translation, 1986.

Chandler, Russell. *Understanding the New Age* (Irving, CA: Word, 1988).

Dickason, C. Fred. *Demon Possession and the Christian* (Chicago, IL: Moody Press, 1987).

Foster, Richard. *Celebration of Discipline* (New York, NY: Harper & Row, 1978).

Friesen, James. *Uncovering the Mystery of MPD* (San Bernardino, CA: Here's Life, 1991).

Garrett, Susan R. *The Demise of the Devil* (Minneapolis, MN: Fortress, 1989).

Garrison, Mary. *How to Conduct Spiritual Warfare* (Hudson, FL: Box 3066, 1980).

Gibson, Noel and Phyllis. *Evicting Demonic Squatters and Breaking Bondages* (Drummoyne, NSW, Australia: Freedom in Christ Ministries, 1987).

Good News Bible. The Bible in Today's English Version (Nashville, TN: Nelson, 1976).

Goodman, Felicitas D. *How about Demons?* (Bloomington, IN: Indiana Univ., 1988).

Green, Michael. *I Believe in Satan's Downfall* (Grand Rapids, MI: Eerdmans, 1981).

Greenwald, Gary L. *Seductions Exposed* (Santa Ana, CA: Eagle's Nest Publications, 1988).

Groothuis, Douglas R. *Unmasking the New Age* (Downers Grove, IL: Inter-Varsity, 1986). *Confronting the New Age* (Downers Grove, IL: InterVarsity, 1988).

Hammond, Frank and Ida Mae. *Pigs in the Parlor* (Kirkwood, MO: Impact Books, 1973). *Demons & Deliverance in the Ministry of Jesus* (Plainview, TX: The Children's Bread Ministries, 1991).

Harper, Michael. *Spiritual Warfare* (Ann Arbor, MI: Servant, 1984).

Kallas, James. *The Satanward View* (Philadelphia, PA: Westminster, 1966). *Jesus and the Power of Satan* (Philadelphia, PA: Westminster, 1968).

Kelly, Bernard. *The Seven Gifts* (London: Sheed and Ward, 1941).

Kinnaman, Gary D. *Overcoming the Dominion of Darkness* (Old Tappan, NJ: Revell, 1990).

Koch, Kurt. *Between Christ and Satan* (Grand Rapids, MI: Kregel, 1962, 1971). *Occult Bondage and Deliverance* (Grand Rapids, MI: Kregel, 1970). *Demonology Past and Present* (Grand Rapids, MI: Kregel, 1973). *Occult ABC* (Grand Rapids, MI: Kregel, 1986).

Kraft, Charles H. *Christianity with Power* (Ann Arbor, MI: Servant, 1989). Inner Healing and Deliverance tapes (Intercultural Renewal Ministries, Box 2363, Pasadena, CA 91102).

Larson, Bob. *Satanism* (Nashville, TN: Nelson, 1989).

Linn, Dennis and Matthew. *Healing Life's Hurts* (New York, NY: Paulist Press, 1979). *Deliverance Prayer* (New York, NY: Paulist Press, 1981).

MacMullen, Ramsay. *Christianizing the Roman Empire* (New Haven, CT: Yale, 1984).

MacNutt, Francis and Judith. *Praying for Your Unborn Child* (New York, NY: Doubleday, 1988).

Mallone, George. *Arming for Spiritual Warfare* (Downers Grove, IL: Inter-Varsity, 1991).

McAll, Kenneth. *Healing the Family Tree* (London: Sheldon Press, 1982).

Montgomery, John W., ed. *Demon Possession* (Minneapolis, MN: Bethany, 1976).

Murphy, Ed. *Spiritual Warfare.* A tape series with workbook. (Milpitas: Overseas Crusades, 1988). "From My Experience: My Daughter Demonized?" in *Equipping the Saints*, (Vol 4, No 1, Winter 1990, 27-29).

Nevius, John R. *Demon Possession* (Grand Rapids, MI: Kregel, 1894, 1968).

Payne, Leanne. *The Healing Presence* (Wheaton, IL: Crossway, 1989).

Peck, M. Scott. *People of the Lie* (New York, NY: Simon & Schuster, 1983).

Penn-Lewis, Jessie. *War on the Saints* (9th ed). (New York, NY: Thomas E. Lowe, 1973).

Peretti, Frank. *This Present Darkness* (Wheaton, IL: Crossway, 1986). *Piercing the Darkness* (Wheaton, IL: Crossway, 1989).

Powell, Graham and Shirley. *Christian Set Yourself Free* (Westbridge, B.C.: Center Mountain Ministries, 1983).

Pullinger, Jackie. *Chasing the Dragon* (Ann Arbor, MI: Servant, 1980). *Crack in the Wall* (London: Hodder and Stoughton, 1989).

Reddin, Opal, ed. *Power Encounter* (Springfield, MO: Central Bible College, 1989).

Rockstad, Ernest. *Demon Activity and the Christian* (Andover, KS: Faith & Life Publications). *Triumph in the Demons Crisis* (Cassette series, Andover, KS: Faith & Life Publications, 1976).

Sandford, John and Paula. *The Transformation of the Inner Man* (So. Plainfield, NJ: Bridge, 1982). *Healing the Wounded Spirit* (Tulsa, OK: Victory House, 1985).

Scanlan, Michael and Randall J. Cirner. *Deliverance from Evil Spirits* (Ann Arbor, MI: Servant, 1980).

Seamands, David. *Healing for Damaged Emotions* (Wheaton, IL: Victor, 1981). *Putting Away Childish Things* (Wheaton, IL: Victor, 1982). *Healing of Memories* (Wheaton: Victor, 1985). *Healing Grace* (Wheaton, IL: Victor, 1988).

Shaw, James D. and Tom C. McKenney. *The Deadly Deception* (Lafayette, LA: Huntington House, 1988).

Sherman, Dean. *Spiritual Warfare for Every Christian* (Seattle, WA: Frontline, 1990).

Shuster, Marguerite. *Power, Pathology, Paradox* (Grand Rapids, MI: Zondervan, 1987).

Subritzky, Bill. *Demons Defeated* (Chichester, England: Sovereign World, 1985).

Sumrall, Lester. *Demons: The Answer Book* (Nashville, TN: Nelson, 1979).

Tapscott, Betty. *Inner Healing through Healing of Memories* (Kingwood, TX: Hunter Publishing, 1975, 1987).

Unger, Merrill. *Biblical Demonology* (Chicago, IL: Scripture Press, 1952). *Demons in the World Today* (Wheaton, IL: Tyndale, 1971). *What Demons Can Do to Saints* (Chicago, IL: Moody Press, 1977).

Wagner, C. Peter. *Engaging the Enemy* (Ventura, CA: Regal, 1991).

Wagner, C. Peter and F. Douglas Pennoyer, eds. *Wrestling with Dark Angels* (Ventura, CA: Regal, 1990).

Warner, Timothy M. *Spiritual Warfare* (Wheaton, IL: Crossway, 1991).

White, Thomas B. *The Believer's Guide to Spiritual Warfare* (Ann Arbor, MI: Servant, 1990).

Wimber, John. *Power Healing* (San Francisco, CA: Harper & Row, 1987).

Worley, Win. *Diary of an Exorcist* (Lansing, IL: Box 626, 1976).

Index

251

Another Book of Interest by Charles H. Kraft

Christianity with Power
Your Worldview and Your Experience of the Supernatural

Power. Politicians crave it. Money buys it. And some people will do anything for it.

In a world where New Agers rely on crystals and channeling to tap into spiritual power, the Christian is reminded that Jesus used supernatural power to heal the sick, cast out demons, and raise the dead. Two thousand years later, the world still desperately needs a Savior who works in power. Charles Kraft believes that many modern Christians have become embarrassed and reluctant to preach a gospel accompanied by supernatural power. Our Western worldview conditions us to fit God into a neat, predictable mold.

But Dr. Kraft is convinced that the power of the gospel will not be confined to our categories. Step by step, he offers a biblical understanding of signs and wonders and shows how Christians can become God's instruments to heal the sick, to work miracles, and to oppose the counterfeit powers of this age. *$8.99*